Cutting-Edge

Art Quilts

Mary W. Kerr

Schiffer Publishing Ltd®

4880 Lower Valley Road • Atglen, PA 19310

Dedication

To the artists who bring out the best in each of us. Thank you to my children, Katherine, Sean and Ryan … all talented artists who are my constant source of inspiration.

Acknowledgments

I thank all the artists who worked with me on this amazing project. Their willingness to share their many talents has resulted in an uplifting, encouraging manuscript that I hope will inspire artists at all phases in their quilting journey.

Thank you to my editor, Jennifer Marie Savage, and the staff at Schiffer Publishing, Ltd., for their unending encouragement and support. And last, but not least, thank you to my family and to the women in my life who serve as my army of cheerleaders. Life would not be the same without you!

Other Schiffer Books by the Author:

A Quilted Memory:
  Ideas and Inspiration for Reusing Vintage Textiles,
  978-0-7643-3921-9, $19.99

A Quilt Block Challenge: Vintage Revisited,
  978-0-7643-3457-3, $24.99

Copyright © 2013 by Mary W. Kerr
Unless otherwise noted,
all images are the property of the author.
Library of Congress Control Number: 2012956080

Designed by Stephanie Daugherty
Type set in Bickley Script LET/Clarendon LT Std/Minion
  Pro
ISBN: 978-0-7643-4313-1
Printed in China

Published by Schiffer Publishing, Ltd.
4880 Lower Valley Road
Atglen, PA 19310
Phone: (610) 593-1777; Fax: (610) 593-2002
E-mail: Info@schifferbooks.com

For the largest selection of fine reference books on this and related subjects, please visit our website at:
www.schifferbooks.com.
You may also write for a free catalog.

This book may be purchased from the publisher.
Please try your bookstore first.

We are always looking for people to write books on new and related subjects. If you have an idea for a book, please contact us at:
proposals@schifferbooks.com.

Schiffer Books are available at special discounts for bulk purchases for sales promotions or premiums. Special editions, including personalized covers, corporate imprints, and excerpts can be created in large quantities for special needs. For more information contact the publisher.

In Europe, Schiffer books are distributed by
Bushwood Books
6 Marksbury Ave.
Kew Gardens
Surrey TW9 4JF England
Phone: 44 (0) 20 8392 8585; Fax: 44 (0) 20 8392 9876
E-mail: info@bushwoodbooks.co.uk
Website: www.bushwoodbooks.co.uk

Contents

Introduction

There has never been a more exciting time to be a quilter or a lover of beautiful quilts. In the past quarter century, our quilt community has expanded in both style and technique, giving birth to a diverse and exciting new category of quilts. Our circle has expanded to include many different voices and talents and we are now able to appreciate all forms of textile art. As quilters, we can embrace our heritage of exquisite bed coverings while celebrating the new techniques, colors, and movement of contemporary Art Quilts.

This book presents a sampling of the considerable talent present in our Art Quilt community today. The work has been divided into six distinct chapters and, while each artist introduces their work, the quilts they share speak for themselves. Where appropriate, artists have shared tips, design processes, and techniques. They have come together to share their love of craft and encourage others in the field of textile art.

Quilt dimensions are given in inches, and contact information is presented for each artist. The reader is invited to visit the various websites to learn more about their work and new creations. This is an exciting field and new and innovative styles and techniques are emerging every day. What we have been able to present here is just the tip of a most creative iceberg!

Enjoy!

Moth Fairy by Julie Duschack.

One: Color Play

Color is the basic building block for every imaginable art form. Nowhere is this more evident than in the diverse world of quilting. Traditional, contemporary, and art quilters alike are first drawn to the colors that are so generously shared in our creations. As artists we celebrate the vast array of choices we find in fibers. We bask in the richness of a hand-dyed wool, enjoy the subtle colors of a painted cotton, and gently caress the beautiful silks. Color brings us together as we create our unique pieces in our signature styles. Whether we embrace every imaginable hue or celebrate the absence of color, the visual feast gives us pause and invites us in for a closer look.

In 2010, I was invited to participate in the Annual Pilgrim and Roy Challenge …. artists create quilts that will be auctioned to raise money for The National Quilt Museum in Paducah, Kentucky. This year, each artist was given a selection of Kaffe Fassett fabrics and allowed to add only two other colors. I chose vintage red and white and created *A Star in the Garden*. I was able to add my vintage palate to a bold contemporary style. I loved working with the unfamiliar colors and enjoyed the stretch of creative fingers. This quilt is now part of a private collection in Portland, Oregon.

A Star in the Garden,
2010,
30 x 30,
Mary Kerr.

Changing Colors, 2007, 19.5 x 24.5 x .5.

Holly Altman

Santa Fe, New Mexico   oaxacamamma@earthlink.net

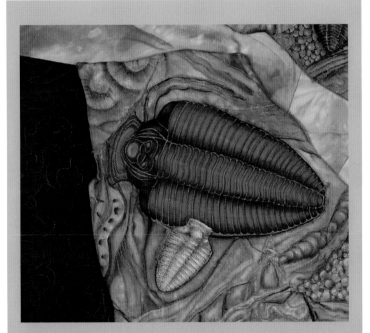

My Process

Though I've worked two-dimensionally for much of my artistic life, art quilting liberates me to play and create in 3-D. Once an idea resolves itself, usually after a number of sketches, I am not only thinking about the image, but about how three dimensions can breathe life into the narrative.

I call this the construction phase. Yet, it's also about de-constructing — because to build, I need first to take everything apart in my mind. Sculpting fabric in three dimensions challenges on many levels.

I play with colors, fabrics, and alternative materials, like Crayola® Model Magic®, which feels like marshmallow, but dries hard enough to cut, sand, and sew. Pipe cleaners and wire often serve as building blocks. There's a lot of trial and error, as I try to balance the tension between the flat, two-dimensional plane of the quilt and the objects trying to break free of the surface.

Artist's Statement

Some people are born with silver spoons in their mouths. I was born with a pencil. From an early age, I could draw with growing precision whatever I saw or imagined. As time passed, precision gave way to interpretation. This phase of my creative career is most evident in my muse: the timeless but ever-changing nature.

Nature nourishes and inspires. In the tumult of today's headlines, the thrall of technology and the tempo of life at the speed limit, nature is the antidote — a source of harmony and order, richness and balance. Nature invites me, in its measured unfolding, to slow down and carefully consider what's before the mind and eye.

I will not be the first or last to call nature my refuge from chaos. The spiral of a chameleon's tail, the growth lines of a seashell, eons-old flora entombed in stone — these remind me that nature worries not about deadlines, market efficiencies, or the swirl of past, present, and future. Nature, for me, exists as a perfect but momentary story of color, texture, and form.

Nature, though I sometimes wish otherwise, provides no blueprints. I hesitate to say I invent techniques, because so much has come before in the art quilt realm. Yet, invent I do — transforming cloth to rock, shell, skin, ceramic, feathers, and other elements needed to make the story spring to life in 3-D. I am, and not least, as much a tinkerer as a quilter. No longer am I limited to saying, "If I can see it, I can draw it." Rather: "If I can think it, I can *make* it."

Koi Rising,
2008,
40.5 x 31 x .75.
Photography by
Carolyn Wright.

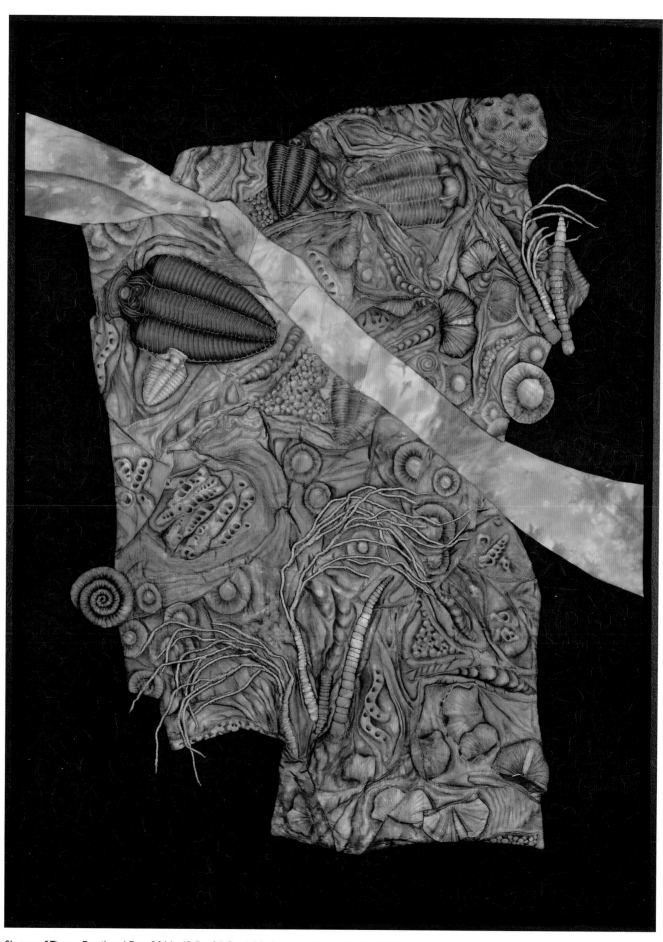

Shapes of Time - Fossil and Fire, 2011, 42.5 x 31.5 x 1.25. Photography by Carolyn Wright.

Dilly Dally,
2011,
43.5 x 68.5.
Photography by
Paul Depre.

Mickey Depre

Oak Lawn, Illinois

www.mdquilts.com

Creative Tip: Change up the scale of a simple image and play with it. A very simple design can become spectacular. By adding one intricate detail, in this case the small fused "x's" for pattern and weight to the flower centers, you make that detail really shine. Sometimes less is truly more.

Artist's Statement

Textiles have always fascinated me. From vintage to current, my taste has always been ALL! Sewing in general, mending to garment making, was never a chore, but, when I pushed myself beyond traditional quilt making, I found the road less traveled was greatly inviting.

My quilts have been described as whirlwinds of color, with oranges residing next to purples of all shades in harmony. Dots, swirls, and stripes intermingle with florals and prints in an outlandish yet exciting visual parade: This is how I see the world and how I want the world to see me.

My work mixes traditional quilting techniques with bold, innovative machine appliqué and threadwork. Fabric choices include my own hand-dyed cotton with commercial cottons for a special spark of color and depth. Pieces are heavily machine quilted.

The images are meant to spark thought and a smile, as humor is a great gift to share.

Fish Kabobs, 2011, 69 x 49. *Photography by Paul Depre.*

Sew Easily Swayed #22, 2010, 42.5 x 25.5. *Photography by Paul Depre.*

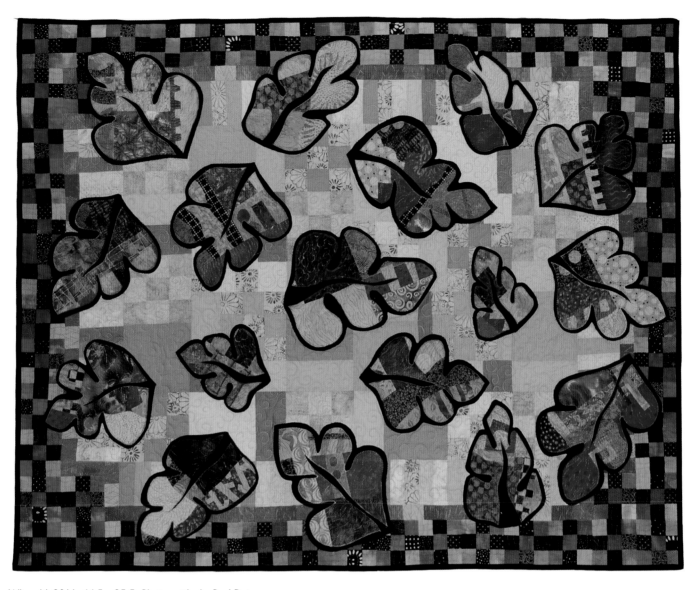

Whoosh!, 2011, 44.5 x 35.5. Photography by Paul Depre.

Creative Tip: You never know what image, sound, or spoken phrase will send your creative muse into play. ALWAYS write or sketch these muses immediately. They have a way of escaping otherwise.

Creative Tip: If you love the traditional method of piecing blocks, incorporate that into your art quilts. I find that more and more I am joining both traditional and nontraditional in my work — and my heart is happy.

Run Birdies Run, 2006, 47 x 26.

Monk in the Doorway, 2010, 74 x 49.

Julie Duschack

Julie Duschack

Denmark, Wisconsin

www.julieduschack.com

Artist's Statement

 I am attracted to quilting and fiber arts above all other art mediums because of the endless potential of layering and transparency.

The layers of fabric and patterns can create complex layers of meaning within the piece. Opaque fabrics can be layered to give the illusion of perspective. Transparent fabrics add another dimension, as do repeating commercial patterns over-dyed to create a new harmonious whole. Quilting, thread painting, and beading are the final touch to a medium with surprising depth.

I have always been fascinated by two recurring themes. The first is our spiritual journey and all of the miracles we must surely be missing as we focus on jobs, laundry, and getting the kids off to school. Secondly, I love sly humor that sneaks up on you, whether it's a technical joke, such as the impossible arches built into *Alian Mountains* or birds with teeth as seen in *Run Birdies Run*. Humor in quilts is always enjoyable, but humor that sneaks in when you're not expecting it is especially fun.

A lot of my work deals with what I suspect are the details we just don't catch as we're busy with our daily lives. If we weren't folding laundry, getting the kids to bed, getting the kids back up again for school, what else would we see? Later, roles shift and shift again. We find ourselves wondering how they can possibly be old enough to drive and yet can't seem to find the laundry room, but we're still rushing.

However, if we could take the time to not only smell the roses but also check under the hostas in our own backyard, what else would we see? What else would we notice?

Alian Mountains, 2006, 18 x 45.

My Technique

I use a combination of my personal photography, drawing, and photo editing tools to accomplish each design. Sometimes it's helpful to use all three tools more than once in the process. For example, start with a photo, develop the drawing, and use Photoshop, or Photoshop Elements, to test the design, the colors, and the quilting lines and then when the main components start to be completed, it's sometimes fun to take a work-in-progress shot and drop that finished section back into the line drawing to double-check the plan once more.

You can test one hundred colors on the computer without messing up your studio. With Photoshop layers, it's like taking an eye exam where the doctor says "do you like A or B" or "do you like B or C." I love designing this way. It saves me having to pay my kids to help me put the studio back in order because I pulled out eight tubs of fabric, which all need to be refolded. It also saves me from dyeing fabric only to find out a different color family would be better. I'm not one of those people who loves dyeing so much that they set aside days and pump out the fabric. I dye for each specific quilt, dyeing, rinsing, drying, ironing, and then making a decision. Am I happy or do I need to do it again?

I certainly save all the pieces that ultimately are not selected, but when I want a new background I always seem to want something just a bit different than what I already have.

I dye mostly cottons, with some rayons, silks, and velvets. Lately, I have found that over-dying batiks offers a richness of pattern that I can't get on my own. I'm sure I *could*, but I'm not willing to practice piano four hours a day either just so I can play beautiful music, so I'm happy to take the dyeing shortcut and work with the lovely patterns already built into many of the batiks.

For me, working through the design decisions is the joy. The sewing is a lot of hard work with brief moments of inspiration, pleasure, and terror. Every quilt seems to go through the "whoever thought this was a good idea" stage as if there is someone else in the studio I could blame for the ugly stages every quilt passes through.

Ultimately, though, fiber is a wonderful medium, with a richness and complexity all of its own.

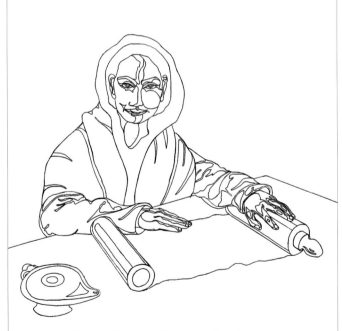

Hulda series, 2003, 24 x 24.

Models for Art Quilters

There are some great resources for artists without access to nude models. Pose File books are more difficult to find now, at least reasonably priced, but are wonderful books. However, even when you can find a pose you like, the figure might be 3" tall. You can rarely see the fingers, the feet, or the ears.

To supplement this type of design, I find handy body parts wherever I can. For the Moth Fairy, I perched my youngest son on a low cabinet and took photos of his hands and feet in various positions. He thinks I destroyed the photos, but of course I didn't. He's posed in his underwear so I won't publish them, but when he's forty years old and hopefully has the good sense to be able to laugh at himself, I plan on printing those photos on fabric and sewing them next to the label on the back of the quilt.

Moth Fairy, 2003, 70 x 59.

Ginkgoes Galore, 2010, 35 x 35.

Ann Fahl

Mount Pleasant, Wisconsin

www.annfahl.com

Artist's Statement

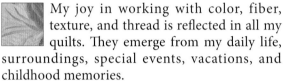 My joy in working with color, fiber, texture, and thread is reflected in all my quilts. They emerge from my daily life, surroundings, special events, vacations, and childhood memories.

Combining a patchwork background gives visual complexity to my simple fused and appliquéd subjects while mixing techniques provides me with unlimited freedom and flexibility to create a variety of effects. It also creates a canvas for my machine embroidery and lush quilting. I feel like I'm dancing and my heart soars when I see wonderful patterns developing on the surface of my quilts. This is when everything comes together!

The same images turn up over and over again. This repetition is a comfort to me. Most of them are from nature: leaves, flowers, my cat, even drinking tea shows up in them from time to time. I do this because I love the image or the feeling it gives me as well as how it works in my composition. I was brought up in a family of classical musicians and an important part of my musical heritage is to practice over and over until you get it right! That is why I create in this manner.

Nothing stirs my imagination more than a big pile of fabric and a little snippet of an idea that comes right from the moment!

Hearts and Trillium,
2011, 17 x 16.5.

Sewn Together, 2009, 33 x 25.5.

Spring Gift, 2010, 48 x 54.

Tri-step Appliqué

The flowers in *Spring Gift* are machine appliquéd in place using a new stitch that I developed called tri-step appliqué. It is based on my free-motion embroidery stitching and creates an extremely wide stitch that covers the edges as opposed to the narrow ridge a satin stitch creates. It creates a soft subtle edge and can be made as wide or narrow as desired.

Floating Flower Scroll, 2002, 106 x 84. Photo by Gregory Case Photography.

Cara Gulati

San Rafael, California

www.DoodlePress.com

Artist's Statement

My fiber art quilt designs start as doodles. Vibrant color is a very important part of my work. More is better in my world. I find that the absence of color, or negative space, is a great way to pop my designs with black fabric. I use lots of curves to create movement and excitement. Threadwork holds three layers together and adds another dimension to the artwork. One of my favorite jobs is making very large art quilts. I use an A-1 long arm quilting machine to quilt my work. I feel I have one of the best jobs in the world!

Colossal Scrolls, 2002, 87 x 110. *Photo by Gregory Case Photography.*

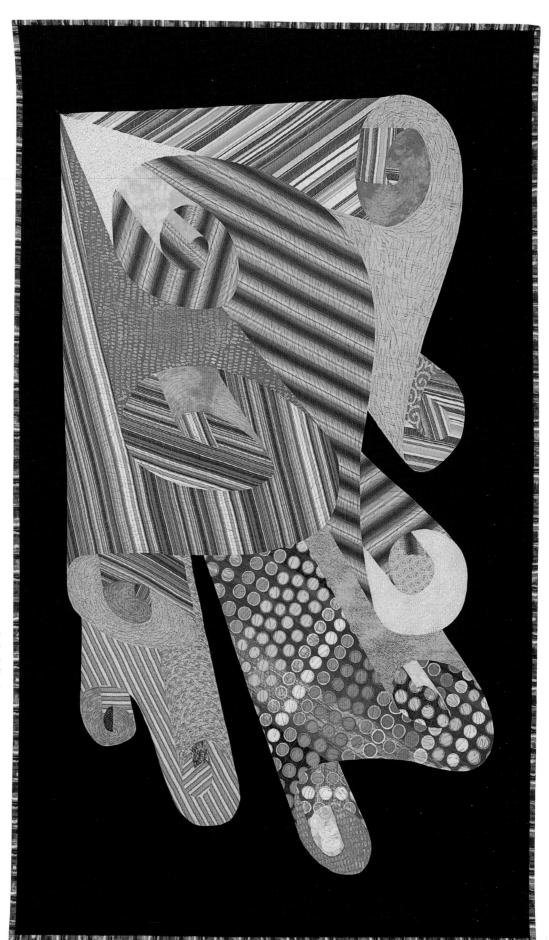

Magna Cum Laude,
2006,
36 x 60.
Photo by Gregory Case
Photography.

Fluttering Flowers, 2009, 24 x 35.
Photo by Gregory Case Photography.

Technique:
Freezer paper templates and machine appliqué

When creating my 3-D Explosion quilts, I play with drawing "S" shapes and add perspective to make the design pop. I use an overhead projector to transfer my designs onto the freezer paper. Next, I cut the templates apart. The shiny side of the template will bond temporarily to the back of the fabric when you press it with a dry iron. Each fabric-covered template is cut out with a seam allowance of fabric that extends beyond the freezer paper template edges. The templates end up sewn back together into the same design that was drawn before it was cut apart. Each seam that meets is appliquéd together. One edge of seam allowance is turned under along the template edge and laid on top of the template it is sewn to. Using a light box, the templates are lined up and held together with masking tape and then stitched on a sewing machine using invisible thread. When the design is completely sewn back together, it will be appliquéd to a background fabric. The background fabric that is behind the appliqué will be cut away, exposing the paper templates, which are then removed. The quilt is then layered with batting and a backing and quilted through all three layers.

The scroll designs resemble a paper that rolls up on both ends. One side looks like a pattern or a stripe. The other side is a color, which is represented by a gradation of a color with a selection of fabrics from dark to light. As the scrolls roll up in different directions, you can see both "sides" alternate, creating the illusion of three dimensions.

Compartments #1, 2011, 32 x 27.

Aryana B. Londir

New River, Arizona

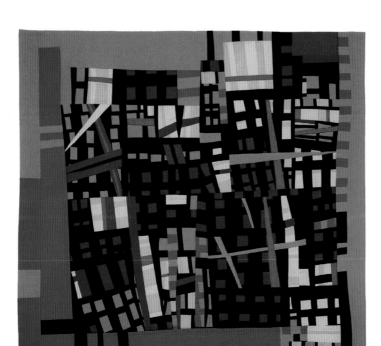

Compartments #2, 2010, 42 x 40.

Artist's Statement

As an artist, I see great value in working in a series. As each piece goes from concept through construction, I am able to explore options and answer the challenges that were not originally explored; new possibilities create themselves as the series continues. Although each piece in a series has a distinct relationship to the other, each also has a distinct personality and individuality that is readily apparent to the viewer.

The "Compartments" series, of which there are two, relates to the compartmentalized living spaces and arrangements found in large cities and poverty-stricken areas throughout the world. The loss of land space to construct dwellings has resulted in the construction of buildings upward as opposed to outward. The view represented in this piece is from above looking down into the spaces.

The "Connections" series was created in order to explore the possibilities of the life-changes that would occur due to missed or broken connections between humans and their existence: Where would I be if I hadn't made that left turn? What would I be doing if I had married someone else? What kind of work would I have performed had I studied elsewhere? Connections change our stations in life and our decisions on how, where, and what our lives become. Everything matters. There is no preset number of pieces to fill a series; it continues until all the challenges, questions, and possibilities are met. Oftentimes, a new series is the by-product of an existing one.

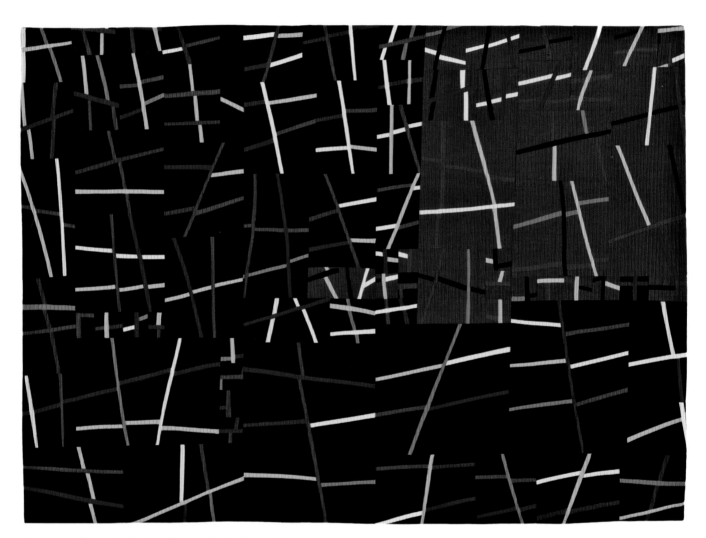

Connections #4, 2011, 48 x 36. Photography by Gregory Case.

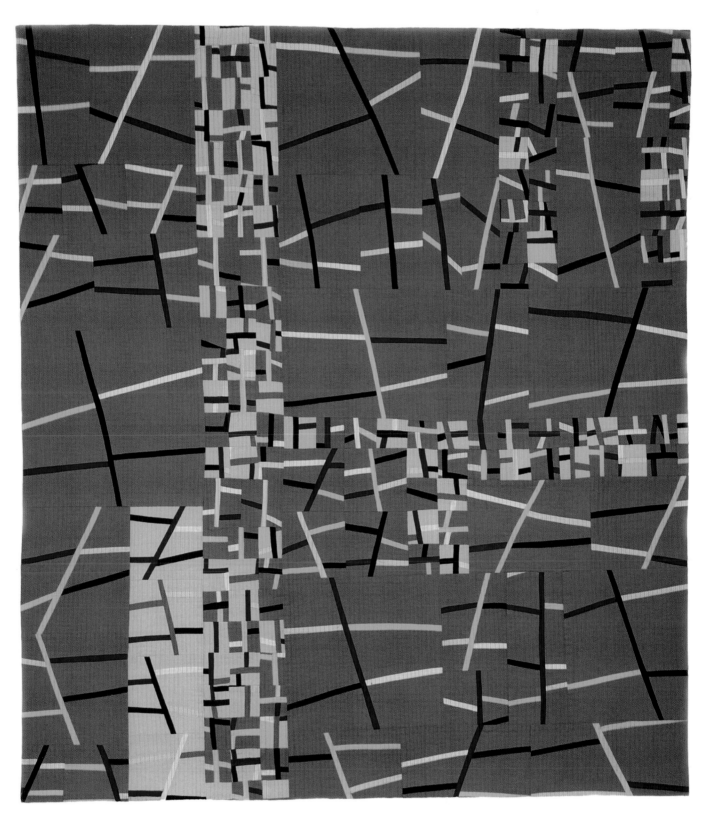

Connections #2, 2010, 47 x 44.

In Deep Thought, 2010, 39 x 39. Photography by Jabari Lumumba.

Aisha Lumumba

Atlanta, Georgia

www.obaquilts.com

Lady Sings, 2010, 36 x 49. *Photography by Jabari Lumumba.*

Second Line Dancer, 2008, 45 x 29. *Photography by Jabari Lumumba.*

Artist's Statement

I want my work to reflect my great African heritage as well as the ups and downs of our American experience. I was born in McDonough, Georgia, and became interested in art at a very early age. I learned to quilt just by watching the elders in my childhood make quilts.

I never planned to be an artist. I simply loved participating in any procedure where I used my hands. I found my interest leaning towards fabrics and the way textiles spoke to me in a musical voice. The colors, designs, and textures moved in and out with a special rhythm.

I strive to capture that musical movement with every piece I create. As the years have passed, I find music and rhythm to be more valuable to my work. I reflect it in my quilts and outwardly in my own voice through my quilt stories. I tell stories at many of my exhibits. I love to create from traditional quilt patterns as well as contemporary designs. I want that mixture to touch a healing spot somewhere deep inside the viewer. I try all kinds of techniques and work hard to go outside my own box. The quilters of Gees Bend have influenced me to go outside the box and explore the freedom from set patterns.

I like to use colors that dance like the gold-orange setting sun over the Serengeti, the green grasses swaying on the Nubian Savannahs, or the bright pink hibiscus blossoms kissing the Caribbean breeze. I hear that same music as the colors and designs all come together. I want the viewer to first feel and then hear the strength of that rhythm. Surely, I want my quilts to tell a story and maybe even SING!

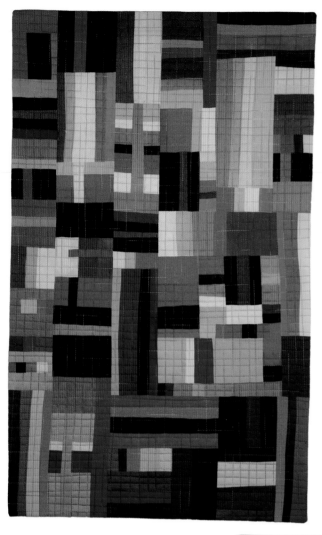

This Way and That,
2009,
33 x 20.
Photography by
Zak Melms.

Sharp Crayons,
2008,
48 x 32.
Photography by
Chris Arend.

Chroma Stack #3,
2008,
26 x 29.
Photography by
Zak Melms.

Diane Melms

Vivid Encounter, 2010, 22 x 28. Photography by Zak Melms.

My Design Process

To keep things interesting, I vary my approach to creating compositions. I also utilize several fabric-piecing techniques, including working directly with shapes, strip piecing and restructuring, and building design with units or motifs. Although I keep a sketchbook of ideas and may start with a simple sketch and palette of colors, much of my composing is done on the wall during the sewing process. Throughout the process, I will freely move units around, switch colors, or make other intuitive adjustments to the composition. It often turns out very different than I first imagined. I love the challenge of manipulating these visual elements to give form to an idea. This intuitive designing is the most engaging part of the quilting process for me.

Artist's Statement

I have been passionate about making art since I was a child. Studying art, teaching art, and learning ways to express my ideas in visual form has been a lifelong pursuit. I feel making art is an essential element to my well-being.

Although I have explored many forms of visual art over the years, I have been repeatedly drawn back to working with fiber. I love fabric! I have been sewing for over fifty years and I'm still enchanted with the material and the process. Many years ago, after leaving full-time employment as an art teacher, I made a serious commitment to my own artistic development with fiber art as my focus and then began a quest to find my creative voice. I have spent long hours in the studio doing serious exploratory work, attending classes, learning to dye my own fabric, exploring the creative possibilities of various design structures, trying new ideas, refining my skills, and building a body of work.

My intent with this work is to create harmonious compositions that communicate feelings or ideas, create a sense of place, a state of mind, or suggest a kind of movement. I love the challenge of working with color relationships, utilizing the expressive qualities of line and shape to suggest a mood, and repeating elements to create patterns that move across the surface.

My passion for working with fabric has grown as I translate what I have learned into my own form of visual expression. I will always aspire to try new ideas, learn more, and push myself to make my art more expressive, interesting, and beautiful.

33

Caladium Study #2,
2007,
41.5 x 43.5.

Susan,
2007,
44 x 40.

BJTitus

Thorndale, Pennsylvania

www.bjtitus.com

Artist's Statement

 Dating as far back as watching my grandmother use her treadle sewing machine, I have had an interest in sewing. After learning to sew from my mother, I honed my skills by studying sewing books and making garments, draperies, and numerous craft items.

Ever since my childhood, I have been intrigued by nature. Over the years I have created numerous flower gardens to display my fervor for flowers and beautiful leafy plants, so it seems only natural that my quilts would reflect this passion.

During the summer months, I tirelessly work in my flower gardens, spending many hours carefully and lovingly admiring nature's beauty. By looking closely at a blossom, you will see many aspects that you might not notice by casting a simple glance.

Most of my quilts are made using a whole cloth background of self-dyed or hand-painted fabric. By dyeing my own fabric I can usually create just what I need. Plus, if it doesn't turn out, it's just another excuse to dye more fabric!

Given our busy schedules in this technology-driven world, I find sanctuary in my sewing studio. Surrounded by fabric, threads, and an awaiting design wall, this is indeed my so-called comfort zone.

While gardening will always remain an important part of my life, my focus now is almost exclusively on quilting. I also enjoy lecturing and teaching my techniques to other quilters — after all, sharing with others and friendship are two of the most important parts of quilting.

Nocturnal Spontaneity, 2002, 60 x 60.

Whimsical Rhapsody, 2004, 41.5 x 43.5.

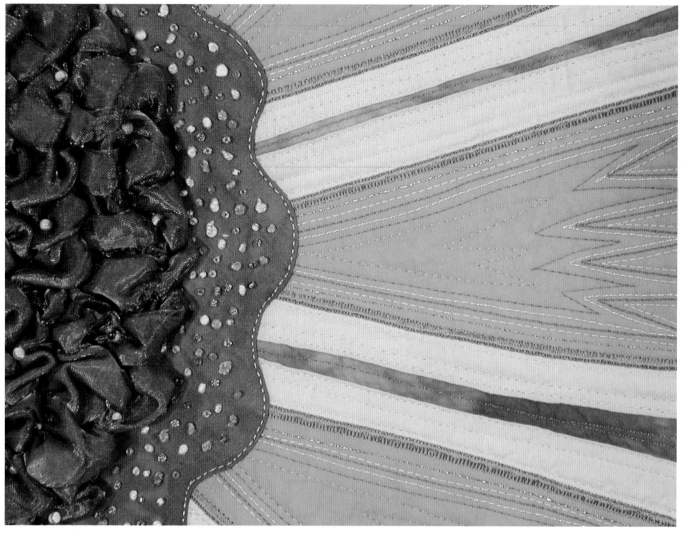

Detail of *Susan*, (see page 34). A close look at the flower's center reveals intricate beadwork.

My Appliqué Techniques

I currently use the following two techniques in most of my quilts: turned-edge appliqué and fused appliqué. Because many of my quilts are handled quite a bit traveling from show to show, I usually satin stitch the raw edge of all the fused pieces. It takes a little longer, but it also eliminates any possibility of fraying and having to "revisit" or touch up portions of the quilt. All threads are knotted and individually buried between the batting and the backing.

I use a standard, domestic sewing machine to appliqué the pieces onto the background. I then complete the quilting using the free-motion method. No fancy stitch regulators are used as I learned to free-motion quilt before they were invented and I have found them to be a bit constraining.

I strive to provide the viewer with a focal point to draw them in for a closer look and then reward them with a surprise. Closer inspection sometimes reveals beadwork, intricate threadwork, or an appliqué feature that cannot be noticed from a distance. However, the viewer is *always* rewarded for taking a closer look.

Two: Alternative Fibers

It is an exciting time to be an art quilter! There are new materials being introduced every year and new ways to incorporate an endless variety of fibers. The rule book has been thrown out and many artists are finding ways to incorporate things that we never dreamed could become an integral part of fiber, cloth, or a quilt. Artists are able to mix and match as never before and are creating combinations that only speak of the possibilities before us.

I chose to work with nontraditional fabrics when I created this compilation piece in honor of my grandmother, Minnie Opal Wilson. Everything I added to this quilt was gathered from her home after her funeral in 2007. I challenged myself to incorporate these unique bits of fiber, trinkets, metal, and even paper into a piece that was as diverse as she was. I love coming from a family where ball fringe can play with antique crochet work and painted linens.

Everything Opal,
2007,
15 x 18.
Mary Kerr.

Ghost Grass, 2011, 46 x 54. Photography by Gerhard Heidersberger.

Glass Garden diptych,
2010,
26 x 108 (each panel).
Photography by
Gerhard Heidersberger.

Katherine Allen

Easton, Maryland

www.KatherineKAllen.com

Night Song, 2009, 19 x 21. *Photography by Gerhard Heidersberger.*

My Design Process

Dampened silk fabric was painted wet and splattered using Golden© and Liquitex© acrylic paints and inks. While the fabric dried, I made a complete tour of the wetlands by my studio, gathering cuttings of everything growing there that day. The specimens were scattered along the salvage edges of the painted fabric laying on my printing table. Medium blue grey Speedball© screen print ink was applied over the painted fabric using my stencil, silk screening technique. Once dry, the printed fabric was cut down the middle, horizontally yielding two very long prints that together could be "read" like a scroll. These two pieces of silk became the whole cloth face layers for two panels that were then attached to backing layers of buckram and hand-stitched throughout.

Artist's Statement

 My artworks are a meditation on nature. I am interested in evoking the keenly joyous moments, celebratory gestures, and expressive colors I find in the natural world. In my tropical garden and studio woodlands, I grow the plant materials used in my creative process. To me, it is important that I am both conceptually and actually partnering with nature in the making of my art.

Each new artwork begins with a canvas of a piece of unstretched cotton or silk. I prepare it by splashing, staining, and painting with water-based pigments. Using a hybrid screen printing and painting process, I enrich the fabric with shapes and lines using live plant materials as stencils. The result is a dense and complex surface. By design, I am never in complete control of this creative process, causing an unpredictable and surprising effect to occur each time. Shapes and lines result from the falling splash of color and the tossing of a leaf or string. These "marks of the moment" capture a beautiful physical logic. My aim is to preserve this residue of the process as much as possible in my finished artwork.

An important philosophy of harmony is often communicated through the co-mingling of the gestures of the human body in motion and the natural forms of growth in the garden. I use threads stitched by hand and machine as both marks of time and to accentuate the serendipitous rhythms developed during the printing process. My goal is to create a piece of art that nourishes the mind, eye, and spirit in equal measure.

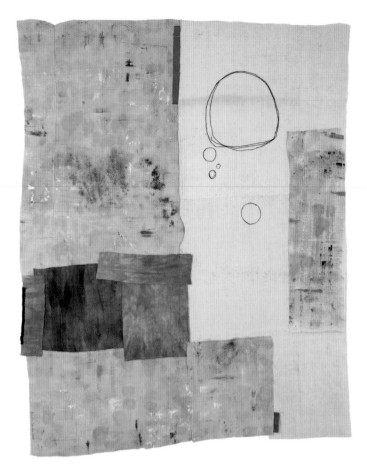

Reflections on a Venetian Wall, 2006, 57 x 47.

Sun Venezia, 2005, 46 x 61.

Night Ride to 1147e,
2011, 150 x 100.

Fanella Davies

North Somerset, England

www.fenelladavies.com

Tracks of a Son, 2010, 8 x 8.

My quilts are abstract in style, both in form and thought, so that I may provide a hint of what might have been. I choose to leave the ultimate definition to the viewer. By concentrating on the textile element of my design, I can incorporate the traces of history and places. Our lives are a mélange of the past and the present — as is the subject of my work.

Artist's Statement

Bold geometric designs and abstract compositions are the central basis of my collaged cloth pieces. I combine vintage cloth, rough linen fabrics, raw and torn edges, and visible stitches with an overlay of dyes and paints, flashing, and scrim. The elements combine to pay homage to the layering of the past and present. I work in series, sometimes three or four at a time; usually one series leads to another.

My pieces are designed to give a sense of place and mood. I pare down my vision to a simple design element — the relationship of form and space. Color and contrast have always been an important element in my work. It is the first visual reference and sets the atmosphere of the work.

41

The Name of a River Can Heal, 2006, each panel 31 x 108. Photography by Paul Elbo.

Eileen Doughty

Vienna, Virginia   www.DoughtyDesignd.com

Currently, my work focuses on exploring what makes textile art so unique from many of the other fine art media: texture, freedom of shape of my "canvas" (using non-rectangular perimeters), and employing three rather than two dimensions.

Artist's Statement

I love the concept of "place" and so my preferred subject matter is the landscape. My background in cartography has been useful in designing my quilts, since designing maps also relies on understanding how people view and interpret colors and symbols. I blend art and science in the creation of my quilts.

The tactile nature of quilts is explored and celebrated in my art. I use "thread sketching" to convey the image into the textile medium, my hands freely moving the fabric as I sew tree branches, leaves, flowers, grasses, and other natural motifs. Details are added with surface design techniques, such as painting, collage, discharging, and stamping, often on nontraditional fabrics.

Taking commissions is one of the best things I have done in my quilting career. I've encountered many color, design, and workmanship challenges that I would never have attempted (or known about) otherwise. My stitching abilities have been enhanced by learning to create artwork sized from very large scale landscapes to postcard-size quilts and even a wearable quilt for a llama.

Welcome Communication, 2002, center panel 56 x 72, side panels 30 x 72. *Photography by Paul Elbo.*

The Anatomy of a Commission

Welcome Communication is a triptych that was commissioned by the Utah Public Art Program and now hangs in the reception area of the Community Center for the Deaf and Hard of Hearing in Taylorsville, Utah. Some of the symbology of the quilt, therefore, relates to sign language and barrier free communication. The circles on the large tree have the manual alphabet drawn on in metallic foil and the ground around the tree has over forty quilted pictorial sign language "words." The words relate to what the patrons of the community center might feel or do while they are there: enjoy, celebrate, welcome, curious, dream, imagine, pleasant, succeed, teach, together, community, challenge, group, interact, advocate/support, and share. The tree itself has branches suggestive of a hand, and similarly there are five roots. The circles flowing between the large tree and the group of distant trees represent barrier free communication.

I learned sign language when I was a cartographer and supervised deaf, hard of hearing, and hearing cartographers. I was delighted to be able to use my knowledge of this wonderful, expressive language again. This was my first large public art commission, which was exciting in itself. The Utah public art administrator was wonderful to work with, as he gave me complete freedom in designing the work. The large space to fill was initially intimidating; I sketched it out full-size on large paper taped to my wall at home — there was only one wall in my house big enough.

The fabrics are a combination of commercial prints, purchased hand-dyes, and ones I painted. I chose colors inspired by that area of Utah and used the color wheel to make them harmonious.

Virginia in the Forest,
2000,
84 x 35.
Photography by
Neil Steinberg.

Moon Dance,
2008,
42 x 51.
Photography by
Miriam Rosenthal.

45

Joie de Vivre,
2010,
48 x 66.

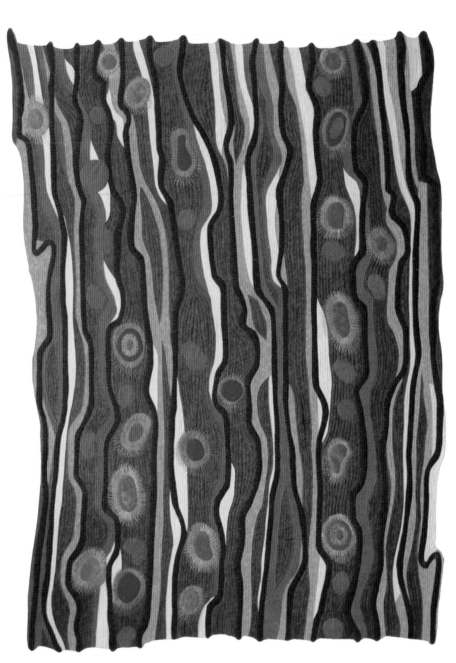

Aglow,
2010,
48 x 45.

Icebergs & Cool Breezes,
2009,
42 x 36.

Anna Hergert

Moose Jaw, Saskatchewan, Canada　　　**www.annahergert.com**

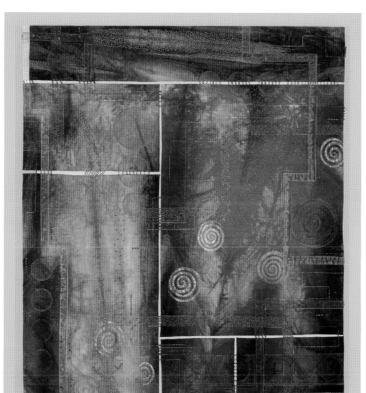

Perpetual Molecular Interconnectivity, 2010, 36.5 × 42.

Creative Tip: *A dye's reaction is dependent upon a number of variables: quality of water, potency of the dye, and environmental temperature all affect the end result. In Perpetual Molecular Connectivity, the straight lines represent the basic rules to follow when embarking on a dye adventure. The spirals introduce the unknown and unpredictable when one or more factors are altered.*

Artist's Statement

Born and educated in Germany, I was exposed to fiber art at an early age. Handwork was a regular part of the weekly school curriculum and my passion for art and textiles became a life-long pursuit.

As an Early Childhood Education graduate, my path rarely took me too far away from creating and sharing new skills in the fiber arts field.

A life-long focus on the arts makes me a passionate and committed artist, teacher, lecturer, and writer. In 2001, I committed to establishing myself as a full-time professional artist. Since 2003, my work has traveled further and visited more exotic countries than I have. Commissions can be found in Canadian, U.S., and European homes and public spaces.

In 2007, my husband and I packed up our household and moved from the big city of Calgary to rural Saskatchewan, where we make our home just north of Moose Jaw at Buffalo Pound Lake. When I am not traveling to lecture or teach, I focus on my art practice in my dream studio overlooking the breath-taking scenery that serves as a constant source of inspiration.

India Revisited, 2011, 32 x 42.

Nita Markos

Hillsboro, Illinois

gmarks@consolidated.com

Developing My Style

I have incorporated several techniques into my signature style. One is the addition of a ghost-like object in the sky; another is the addition of a story theme with wording added to enhance the story; a third is objects separately quilted and then appliquéd onto the background; and, finally, use of paper piecing in the borders. Throughout all of my work, color, line, shape, and space play a part in achieving the mood that I wish the viewer to see and feel.

Artist's Statement

 I have painted and drawn all of my life and began my commercial training by doing illustration for a small publication. I taught art, kindergarten through high school, and only began quilting after I retired and moved to a home on a lake with my husband.

With retirement came a wide range of new experiences, including traveling, gardening, writing, and, most exciting of all, quilting. When a new neighbor invited me to go to her quilt guild, I had no idea how that night would change my life. I was hooked. It was as if I was a closet quilter coming out. I had always been fascinated by fabric, but quilting was foreign to me. I learned quilting skills from my new friends and made two traditional quilts — and then discovered art quilts and it has been my passion ever since.

Inspiration for my quilts has come from many sources. People often ask how long it takes to make a quilt. Actually it takes a lifetime of experience and experimentation.

A television program set me on the road to curved piecing and curved piecing led me to be inspired by nature, specifically my garden flowers. A favorite artist led me to try abstract compositions while travels to India, Africa, Egypt, and China put new ideas, techniques, and inspiration into my creative genes.

Step-by-step, my signature style has evolved. It is personal and fulfilling and I am grateful to all who have encouraged me, including my husband, whose practical mind, sharp observation, attention to detail, and especially patience are ever welcome.

Into the Future, 2010, 42 x 42.

Silver Wings at Midnight,
2008,
16 x 42.

Sunflowers,
2010,
21 x 33.
Photography by
Frank DiPerna.

Quilt Sampler,
2010,
45 x 61.
Photography by
Frank DiPerna.

Niagra Falls,
2010,
24 x 24.
Photography by
Frank DiPerna.

Marjorie Marovelli

Manassas, Virginia (Nov. 24, 1933 - Feb. 21, 2012)

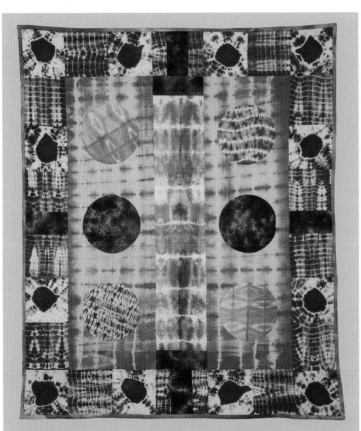

Shibori Circles, 2011, 40 x 48. Photography by Frank DiPerna.

Creative Tip: *To create this Shibori quilt, I used the traditional Japanese hand-tied method to create these tie dyed fabrics. Before dying the fabric, it is folded or tied with a string, rubber bands, clamps; anything that will cause the fabric to resist dye. For the circles, I did stitching with string and larger plastic paper clips. On the borders, I used the stitching technique and on alternate blocks, I wrapped the fabric around a bottle cap and secured it with rubber bands. Then the fabric was dyed with cold water dyes.*

Artist's Statement

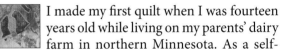

I made my first quilt when I was fourteen years old while living on my parents' dairy farm in northern Minnesota. As a self-taught fabric artist, I have continuously worked with simple materials to create my designs and during the years I raised my five children sewing was an art form that was easily incorporated into my life. I work intuitively with colorful fabrics and I use both geometric forms and organic subject matter to create my quilt images. Color and pattern have always been an integral source for my ideas.

It is a natural process for me to lay out a large array of fabrics and start sorting and placing them next to each other. This is the starting point for the creation of my designs. While I employ the methods of traditional quilting in my work — embroidery and machine stitching for example — I always enhance my pieces with more unconventional surface design techniques, such as hand dyes, marbling, batik, stamping, and hand-painting. This process allows me to explore a more personal and experimental expression in my quilts and utilizes my painting skills that I have always enjoyed.

High Flight, 2006, 61 x 76.

Linda S. Schmidt

Dublin, California

www.shortattn.com

Techniques and Process

This quilt began with a photo my brother took of a Norwegian Fjord where it falls to the sea. I combined this with another photo of an eagle flying to its handler, as well as one I took of a blasted tree in Colorado.

I made tracings from each photo, combined them and made a master drawing, and then enlarged that to two different sizes. I made three of this scene simultaneously — one large piece and two smaller pieces half that size — so I could have one to enter competitions, one to give to my brother, and one for my office. Each fabric piece was individually cut, ironed over freezer paper templates, and then invisibly machine appliquéd onto Totally Stable.

The challenge of creating water that moves and flows, falls, and shimmers is one that I particularly enjoy — and took to rather extreme lengths in this piece. In some places, there is underlying rock, MistyFuse®, roving, and then Angelina® fiber, fused together. Some places are satin and silk fabrics with sheer fabric overlays, some are Tintzl® and Angelina® combined over rocks, and some places are painted melted cellophane and iridescent cracked ice over white fabrics, with a little fabric paint and glitter glue thrown in for good measure. A girl does need a bit of variety, eh?

The eagle was foundation pieced to paper and then machine and hand appliquéd. The tree was drawn onto black batting, felted with yarns and an Embellisher machine, and then appliquéd to the finished background.

Artist's Statement

Quilts are some of my earliest memories — being stuck under them in the dead of winter in South Dakota, giggling there in the quiet darkness because those quilts were so heavy you could not move your toes once you were tucked in. I started my first quilt when I was eight years old, finished it when I was twenty, and have been quilting ever since.

Most of my pieces are combinations of many techniques and textural elements, as I am always searching for better, more interesting ways to bring my visions out into the real world where others can see them.

I make quilts because quilts are my art and fabric is my medium. When I started out, all of my quilts were scrap quilts — quilts made from bits and pieces of the fabric of life, sewn together to make a whole that was far greater than the sum of its parts, for those parts were once a daughter's dress, a Grandma's apron, a memory of a trip, or the robe a priest wore to celebrate Easter mass. The quilts made from those fabrics connect me with all the people who wore, used, or designed them. We make quilts to keep the people we love warm and to create the art that keeps us whole. I rarely use scraps of dresses any more, but it's still all connected for me in quilting — the fabric, the tradition, the making and doing, the learning and trying — all caught up in the attempt to make art that moves and stretches, challenges and changes.

I make quilts because I believe they are important, in and of themselves. In making quilts, we fill empty spaces with beauty and empty hands with comfort — and that is more than a lot of people will ever attempt to do. Mother Theresa once said, "We can do no great things...only small things with great love." That's our job and our joy...that's what we're here for.

55

Roses for Remembrance, 2000, 108 x 100. *Photography by Sharon Risedorph.*

Celebrate the Material World
(front and back views),
2008, 72 x 72.
Photography by Sharon Risedorph.

Rejection, 2008, 20 x 20. Photography by Werner Boeglin.

Maya Schonenberger

Miami, Florida　　　www.mayaschonenberger.com

The Author's Thoughts on "Rejection"

Being rejected is part of every artist's life. For many years I have been contemplating the idea of a "rejection" show, knowing I would be able to pull together a really interesting and high quality exhibition. My show idea inspired the third of the *Yangtze* pieces, called "Rejection." The Chinese calligraphy in the left hand area spells "rejection" in Chinese.

Artist's Statement

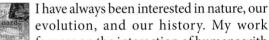 I have always been interested in nature, our evolution, and our history. My work focuses on the interaction of humans with nature and the changes that result from this process. Intrigued by the possibilities that textiles offer, I started exploring different techniques guided by my sense of colors and the feelings they invoked. I strive to be in tune with my mind, body, and surroundings, and continuously search for new ways of expressing my thoughts, feelings, and concerns.

I enjoy working in series. They enable me to work on a subject matter in depth. During the last few years, I created a series called "Urban Sprawl," "Hindsight," and another one titled "Stretched to the Limit." The latter focuses on endangered animal or plant species and social issues. To emphasize my visual art statement, I choose to use a strong narrow horizontal and vertical format.

Living in southern Florida exposes me to more than just lush, rich tropical life and beautiful waters. It also brings brush fires, floods, droughts, spills, and pollution. I watch as south Florida's urban sprawl expands like an uncontrolled brush fire, leaving behind large concrete and asphalt areas as well as polluted waters.

59

*Hindsight,
2008,
20 x 20.
Photography by
Werner
Boeglin.*

Skyline, 2011, 20 x 55. Photography by Werner Boeglin.

Three: Threadwork

Detailed threadwork allows quilters to add yet another beautiful layer of dimension to their work. Hand embellishment with decorative threads, heavy thread play on a domestic machine, creative writings, and long arm magic all embrace the power of thread. Advances in technology have allowed us the opportunity to play with a wide variety of machines, stitches, and techniques. New ideas are swirling as artists continue to push the limits of conventional wisdom.

I created *Tropical Smoothie* when I was exploring new ways to showcase vintage textiles. (Some of my ideas were better than others!) The vintage 1950s fabric was heavily thread painted to enhance the tropical design. I learned quickly that more is better and loved the variety of colorful threads I was able to incorporate in this tiny piece.

*Tropical Smoothie,
2006,
11 x 11,
Mary Kerr.*

Skin Deep,
2011,
46 x 57.
Photography by
Howard Freeman.

Skin Deep II,
2011,
46 x 57.
Photography by
Howard Freeman.

Nancy Billings

Miami, Florida   **www.nancybdesigns.com**

Skin Deep III, 2011, 46 x 57. *Photography by Howard Freeman.*

Artist's Statement

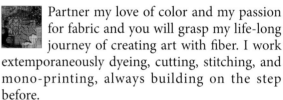

Partner my love of color and my passion for fabric and you will grasp my life-long journey of creating art with fiber. I work extemporaneously dyeing, cutting, stitching, and mono-printing, always building on the step before.

My latest work *Skin Deep* parallels the fabric layers to the many layers of a person's life and the stitching to the many directions and choices we make that can change our destinations. Although each unique mini quilt represents individuals, this work tries to show their overall relationship to each other and the world around us, how we are all sometimes "hanging by a thread."

My work is designed to hang away from the wall so that the fluctuation of wind and air can alter the movement of the squares while projecting shadows on the wall. The reflecting shadows represent the influence of individuals to the world around us.

Wisdom, 2010, 33 x 40.5.

Jennifer Day

Santa Fe, New Mexico

www.jdaydesign.com

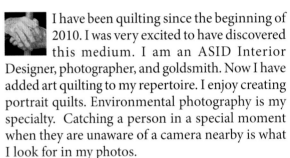

Artist's Statement

I have been quilting since the beginning of 2010. I was very excited to have discovered this medium. I am an ASID Interior Designer, photographer, and goldsmith. Now I have added art quilting to my repertoire. I enjoy creating portrait quilts. Environmental photography is my specialty. Catching a person in a special moment when they are unaware of a camera nearby is what I look for in my photos.

I utilize free motion embroidery in my art. I photograph a subject, print the image onto fabric, and then begin the process of covering the image in thread. My images may have between ten and sixty threads per subject. The process of blending the colors seamlessly together is challenging and time-consuming. When I sit down at my machine, I typically will stitch for five or six hours at a time. Creating a portrait in thread is an intense process. I incorporate free motion quilting into the background of the piece as well as appliqué and many times trapunto.

My art incorporates between one and three million stitches in the finished art quilt. I have used as many as 4200 yards of thread in a single art quilt. My style of thread painting is very intense and the projects may take as long as 150 hours to complete.

65

Siempre Hay Esperanzo, 2011, 26 x 31.

Dream Music, 2010, 44 x 52.

Threadwork Techniques

I love to tell stories in thread and portraits have a lot of stories to tell.

I begin my process with my camera. I spend hours photographing people in everyday circumstances looking for just the right image that will speak to me about how people live. Once I have selected the image to thread paint, I determine the size of the finished quilt. I then print the image onto photo fabric. If I am printing an 8 x 11 or 13 x 19 image, I use EQ Printables. If I am working in a larger format, I use Jacquard Inkjet Fabrics for my photo fabric.

To create my quilt sandwich, I use the photo fabric on top. I then use an 18-ounce canvas behind the photo. I place the photo on the canvas on the bias. By using the bias, I avoid all puckering when intensively stitching the image. The key is the 18-ounce canvas. I then place batting behind the canvas and finish the sandwich with an appropriate backing cloth. I choose a backing that is similar to the predominate color in the photograph. I will stitch through the entire sandwich allowing the threads to be seen on the back of the quilt. I then begin thread painting.

I use a straight stitch in my painting. A tight zigzag can also be used if the end result is a looser portrait. On any machine, using a straight stitch will work for thread painting. A darning foot is essential to this process. I prefer an open toe darning foot so that I can see exactly where the needle is entering the fabric. The feed dogs need to be in the down position. Adjust the height of the darning foot so that it rests about 1/8" above the needle plate on the machine. This will allow you to move the fabric freely under the needle. I use a 90/14 needle for free motion work. The sandwich is heavy due to the 18-ounce canvas, but will move easily. If you are working a large format, you will need to roll the edges of the portrait to fit the fabric through the throat of the machine. A larger — 44" wide quilt — is best stitched using a 10" or larger throat. I also use a sit down Handi-Quilter machine with a 16" throat to finish my quilts.

Old Hands, 2011, 44 x 40.

Koi Dragon, 2011, 27 x 40.

Dusty Farrell

Cambridge Springs, Pennsylvania   www.cscountrystitchin.com

Dusty's Amazing Coat (front and back views), 2011.

Whitetail Morning, 2011, 42 x 32.

Artist's Statement

 I am a quilt artist. I have always considered myself to be artistic. I started painting at about thirteen and took art classes as a high school student where I enjoyed painting wildlife scenery. My paintings provided a second source of income in my early twenties. After becoming unemployed in 2005, I decided to try my luck and find a way to make a living doing what I love. I purchased a Longarm quilting machine in 2005 and opened a quilt shop with my wife Stephanie. After a year or so of practice, working on technique and style, I felt comfortable with my new artistic medium.

I am a Longarm quilt artist who has taken my passion for art and turned it into a new and exciting career. I fill a niche in the quilting and art community by not just thinking outside the box, but also by quilting *outside* the box. In my quilt shop, I am able to make several hundred quilts a year for customers all over the world. I teach the "Imperfect-perfect" in my quilting classes and my students leave with confidence, inspiration, a fresh new look at quilting, and a fearlessness as far as quilting, quilts, and fabric are concerned. I hope to instill in my students that their quilting is more about consistency, flow, and texture than repetition.

My dream is to teach full-time and design and create custom quilts for customers and for show. I plan to continue breaking the rules and barriers of tradition and creating art for all to enjoy and be inspired by. It is an exciting ride!

Moon Over Manhattan,
2010,
34 x 39.

Creative Tip: *One component of the machine quilting process for each of the quilts is serendipity. While I practice a lot both on fabric and paper, when it gets down to the actual quilting I just go for it. I don't think too much. I don't plan. I change thread weights and colors on a whim. I've frequently referred to my process as "short attention span quilting." When I'm ready for a change in motif or color, I just go for it.*

Twilight in the Bronx,
2009,
43 x 43.

Teri Lucas

Bronx, New York

terificreations@gmail.com

Serendipity, 2011, 12 x 12.

I quilt on a Bernina 1080 that I have owned for seventeen years. Because it cannot be fitted with a stitch regulator, I have learned to stitch at a medium speed, which gives me better control and a more consistent stitch length. There is something quite peaceful that happens as I sit at the machine, listening to its rhythm and my intuition when it comes to motifs, thread color, and thread weight.

Artist's Statement

I started out as a traditional quilter choosing traditional patterns and methods — machine-piecing and hand-quilting were for me. This began to change when I joined a local guild and went to my first major quilt show. I began to see the quilt world embracing quilters in a way that welcomes and encourages growth and development.

My quilter life changed when I realized that stitching out motifs on the machine is perfectly acceptable. I began to respond to the endless possibilities of what can be done on the machine that I could not accomplish by hand. Now my mind races with ideas and I dream of what can happen with thread, batting, and fabric. I've doodled for years, practicing quilting motifs and figuring out how to stitch them out and scale them so that they fit the quilt I'm working on. The doodling has changed to thoughtful drawing as I create the quilts I visualize in my head on sketchbook pages, creating memories of the quilts I'd like to make.

The quilt series I'm working on has a traditional feel with a bit of a twist — I use thread to create the traditional elements, i.e. stars, circles, arcs in the quilt. Trapunto is frequently incorporated to give the pieces a bit of depth. I'm working on expanding my color palate by using complimentary colors to really let the stitching tell the story and be present in the quilt.

Clothed in Color, 2011, 36 x 48.

Sarah Ann Smith

Hope, Maine

www.sarahannsmith.com

The Wall, 2007, 27 x 29.5.

Artist's Statement

Color. Line. Texture. Imagery. Stories. Being part of the tradition of quilting and part of the future of quilting and art. The act of creating. Making the pictures in my head become real…. These are some of the things that spur me to create my quilts.

My subject matter varies. At the moment, I am driven to portray the human body. I find the challenge of capturing a representation of a person (or a part of them, like their hands) to be one of the hardest things I could do, and I love it when I actually get the image in my head into the cloth successfully. I am always learning; I've never made a quilt from which I didn't learn a new method (even if it was after the quilt was done, when I think…Oh! Geez…if I had done it that way instead it would have been so much easier).

I do not limit myself to just one technique. I use whatever I need to achieve the desired effect, including dyeing, painting, hand and machine quilting, embroidery, embellishing with beads, yarns, and any suitable object, piecing, and appliqué (hand, machine, raw-edge, fused or not…you name it!), and many more yet to be discovered and tried. I stitch intensively on my home sewing machine with a variety of threads that would make a beginning quilter shudder at the cost!

Cookie? PLEEEZE Cookie!, 2010, 12 x 12.

I loved the techni-color portrait of our family pug and think doing the cats would be fun. I am also feeling a pull to return to some landscape quilts, too. Lurking in the back of my head is the tiny seed of a larger story, to create a new place or world — perhaps infused by the fiction I read and mythologies from various cultures. I'm hoping for time (ever elusive) to let that seed germinate and grow until it is ready to move from the dark confines of my brain and into quilts. Inspiration is everywhere... we just need to be open to receive it and transform it into art.

> **Creative Tip:** *Play with color! The portrait of our pug, is a study in value: light-medium-dark. Although I chose medium values, as I composed the picture I realized that a pug's face doesn't really have medium tones: just light and dark, so his face became oranges and greens (on the light side) and the purples and deep blues. I used my favorite "medium" turquoise color in the background and quilted dog bones into it.*

Joshua, 2010, 36 x 48.

Too Much Soul to Control,
2006,
36 x 36.

We'll Always Have Paris,
detail

We'll Always Have Paris,
2008,
26 x 36.

I'm Just Saying,
2010,
26 x 36.

Cyndi Souder

Annandale, Virginia   **www.MoonlightingQuilts.com**

Time Flies, 2005, 31 x 29. Photography by Third Eye Photography.

Creative Tip: Never underestimate silk organza. I knew I wanted a black background, but that's a lot of real estate to devote to plain black fabric. Instead of using just the plain black cotton, I hand-stamped a layer of grey/silver silk organza with black ink to create some visual interest and then quilted that onto the black cotton. The effect is subtle, but it rewards the viewer who ventures close enough to appreciate it.

Protect your work surface from the ink that will inevitably come through the weave of the organza. Use a fresh inkpad and repeat the stamps for unity and consistency. Simple is best.

Artist's Statement

From vision to reality, everything about the quilt process engages me: the initial flash of inspiration, the fabric choices, the design decisions, and especially the quilting. I love the process.

I have been working with commercial fabric mostly, but that seems to be changing. I like to stamp and layer my own fabric to use as backgrounds and I like to incorporate silks where I can. I also like to work with texture and embellishments, using beads, old clock parts, and trinkets from the home center. I prefer to let the piece tell me what it needs and then I do my best to live up to its expectations.

As a writer and former English teacher, I like to incorporate text in my art. It adds a layer of meaning to each piece and it allows me to use words and letters as graphic elements. Sometimes I quilt the words and letters into the piece using my free motion quilt writing technique. For other quilts, I stamp or stencil the letters onto the surface of the quilt top using paints or ink. Since my non-art interests all involve writing, it seems natural to include writing in my art.

Wondering how to get the lines of text so straight? I used blue painter's tape, one of my favorite quilting tools. I laid it out as a straight edge to keep the baseline of my quilt writing straight. Whenever I had a letter with a descender (tail), I made sure my stitches were nice and small to perforate the tape, making it easy to tear the tape away from the stitching. Since I mitered the corners of the border, I used the seam line as a guide to turn the corner with my quilt writing.

Most often, I make quilts in response to challenges or commissions where I have to conform to a theme, a set of rules, or a client's desires. When my schedule allows, I work with ideas and techniques that make my heart sing. I love structure — trees, buildings, standing stones. I incorporate words wherever I can and I revel in their graphic nature. I believe that black is a neutral and I include it in almost everything.

77

Bargello with Coneflower, 2009, 40 x 31.

Karin Täuber

Blacksburg, Virginia

www.BRQFestival.com

Artist's Statement

I have always loved color and fiber. Painting with thread and making art quilts bring together these passions in exciting and satisfying ways.

My international background inspires my quilting. During my time in college in Munich, Germany, I attended a variety of art classes. I happily worked with many media involving an array of paints, pencils, ceramics, collage objects, paper-making, and jewelry-making, but didn't find the fitting artistic road I wanted to travel. My introduction to quilting in America changed all that.

In quilts, I became intrigued by the geometric patterns and design the fabrics created. I played with many different piecing and quilting techniques as I found my current voice. Recurring themes in my quilts now involve natural configurations: flowers, vines, rocks, trees, and grasses. My inspirations come from many sources, including my own photographs, photography books, calendars, and impressionistic artists such as Claude Monet.

I have found that every time I try something different it just sends me off on a new adventure and broadens my abilities. My quilts are an expression of that journey; sometimes carefully planned, organized, colorful, and complicated while other times they are just happy accidents.

I start most art quilts by using traditional quilting techniques such as traditional blocks, exact seam allowances, mitered borders, and hand appliqué. I then combine them with the more free form "art" techniques of raw edge machine appliqué, extensive machine embroidery, and thread-work, as well as overlays of tulle and organza for shading and depth. Each art quilt is completed using free-motion machine quilting to enhance the design and beading to add sparkle and increase the dimension in the work. I get so caught up in the creative process that I sometimes wake up during the night with ideas about quilts or solutions to new techniques I'm currently exploring.

In the quilting world, there are "traditional quilters" and free-form "art quilters"; I like to describe myself as a "traditional art quilter."

March of the Loggerhead Turtles,
2008,
26 x 56.

Stone Bridge near Laragh, 2011, 37 x 28.

The Creative Process

Working from an original image I drew the quilt in full scale to create a paper foundation. I was captivated by the idea to pixel the trees in the background as well as the water under the bridge. Almost like in a traditional watercolor quilt, squares of different blue or green shades are set on point and pinned to the paper foundation. Contrary to watercolor, however, similar fabrics should be placed next to each other to add more calmness to certain areas. The squares are sewn onto the paper foundation in strip sets.

The bridge was drawn in full scale on the grey fabric. A variety of differently shaded fabrics were used for larger boulders. It is important to gradually shade the boulder colors from light to dark to achieve depth and distance.

I used Roxanne's Glue Baste-It® to temporarily tack the boulders to the bridge shape. I prefer this fabric glue, as the bottle has a wonderful long tip that helps to squeeze a tiny drop under each square fast and easily. The quilt top, layered on a muslin foundation, was then free-motion embellished with the sewing machine and little details like leaves and grass were added with a selection of variegated Superior Threads™. The quilt was layered with Hobbs Thermore Batting and free-motion machine quilted.

Tulle in different shades and colors was placed over the blue fabric squares and tucked in different areas to deepen the effect of rippling and flowing waters. The areas where the water meets the outside edge of the quilts were intentionally left uneven and a long-threaded yarn was added to further intensify the free flowing effect.

America Surrounded,
2010,
70 x 65.
Photo by
Ron McCoy Photography.

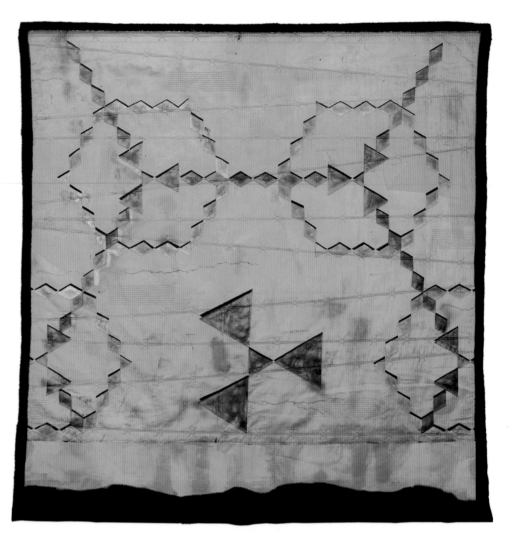

Almost Symmetrical,
2011,
73 x 44.
Photo by
Ron McCoy Photography.

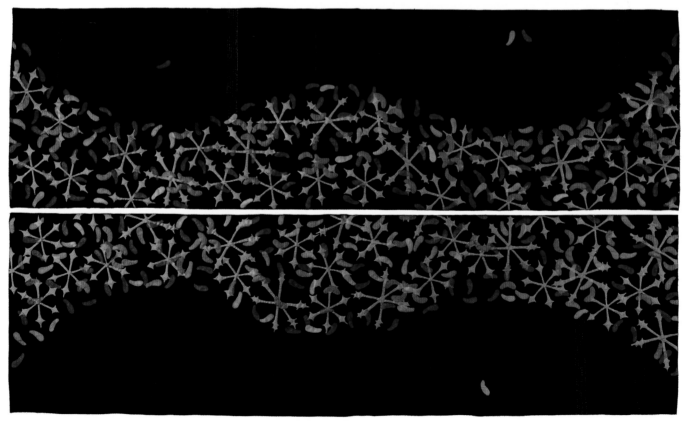

Mary Vaneecke

Tucson, Arizona

www.maryvaneecke.com

Artist's Statement

 I used to believe that a work of art should stand on its own. Lately, I have come to realize that art may, after all, be all about the artist — and the viewer. Learning about the context of a work of art can make me think about it in very different and often more appreciative ways. I love to know about an artist and her thought processes when I look at a piece of art — that context is always important to understanding a work.

I am the eldest of four girls and grew up in a suburb of Detroit. I was dubbed the "smart one" of the family. As such, I neither studied nor practiced art until mid-life. My work comes out of the quilting tradition — quilting and sewing were "safe" pursuits, not because they were "womanly" but because they didn't seem particularly artistic. I had passed junior high home economics, after all, and I thought sewing a quilt didn't require real talent like, for instance, painting a picture did.

When one of my sisters — the one dubbed the "creative one" — suggested a round robin quilt project, I jumped at the opportunity. Within a few years, I opened a longarm machine quilting service in my adopted hometown of Tucson, Arizona.

While quilting for others full-time, I looked for ways to create my own work. Time constraints gave me the impetus to explore non-traditional methods of surface design: painting, discharging, decorative stitching, embellishing, printing, and image transfer. These methods are outside the traditional quilting toolbox and can be faster than hand-stitching miles of invisible appliqué. My mantra became *There are no quilt police* — and I decided not to let anyone tell me how I "should" work.

Most of my work is layered and stitched, which is the technical definition of "quilting," but we are talking form and not function here. My quilting stitches always add a critical design element to a piece; they are integral to my work and are part of the design from the beginning. I frequently start with a solid color fabric to ensure my quilting stitches are the most visible.

My Mother is a Fish, 2006, 24 x 24. Photo by Ron McCoy Photography.

Four: Special Techniques

Quilters are as diverse as their individual makers and each artist brings something new and exciting to the creative community. Some of these artists go above and beyond as they create in a unique style that makes the audience stop, study, and slow down a little to just enjoy. These artists have developed a technique that has not followed the traditional path of quiltmaking; instead, they have figured out how to create in an unusual manner that celebrates their stories and innate abilities. The journey each makes to get to their own "happy creative space" is unique, exciting, and part of the creative process.

Guitar Fish was created for my then-teenage son when his love of music and my passion for quilting (and all things motherly) seemed to be miles apart. Using a Susan Carlson technique, I fussy cut bright musical fabric to create a whimsical fish. The bright composition was overlaid with tulle and machine quilted to celebrate my love for my son and respect for his unique passions.

Guitar Fish, 2006, 24 x 18, Mary Kerr.

Another Form II,
2009,
52 x 42.

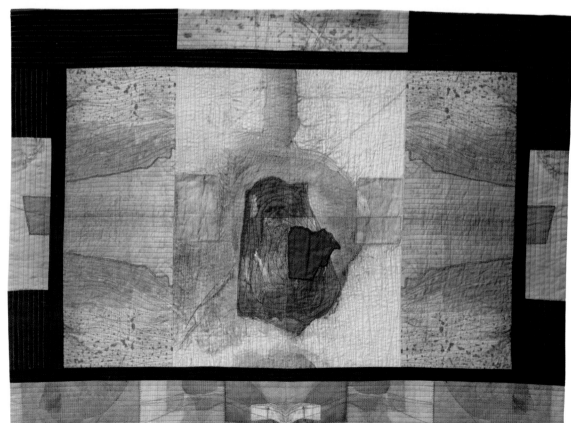

Landscape Revisited I,
2008,
32 x 28.

Peggy Brown

Nashville, Indiana

www.peggybrownart.com

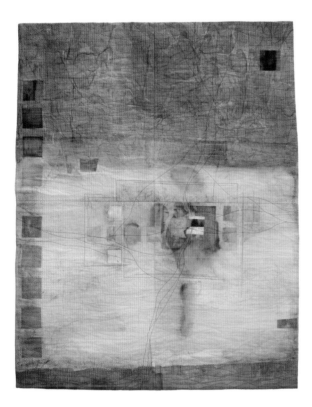

Changes, 2010, 37 x 44.

Artist's Statement

I paint and quilt for myself, for the challenge and joy of it, and because it is something I just have to do. Knowing visual art must be *seen* to be heard, true fulfillment comes when the viewer unites with my vision and becomes a part of my marks on paper or fabric.

My studio time is divided between "paintings on paper" and my newer obsession, "paintings on fabric." Since I have spent over thirty years painting and teaching transparent watercolor painting, it's only natural I approach my art quilts from the viewpoint of a watercolor artist using the same media and methods for both. On a thoroughly wet substrate, either paper or fabric, I brush on paint and allow the pigments to mingle and follow their personal paths as they dry. The resulting image inspires and helps me choose the way to completion. For added texture and to strengthen and define the design, I collage and fuse pieces of paper or fabric over the whole cloth start and then it is re-painted and quilted by machine. Materials in my painted quilts include silk cotton, flannel, interfacing, and various painted papers. My goal is to take a free-flowing start and, using collage, add overlays of more pigment and drawing to compose a well-designed finish.

From tentative beginnings to the final touch, I try to express images that are on, above, and below the surface. By keeping each painted layer transparent, I invite the viewer to follow as I work and perceive the process from tentative beginnings to the final touch. The entire process is a collaboration between the medium and myself. I think we both enjoy ourselves.

My work could be described as experimental. I try to allow experiments to synchronize with my natural ways of painting and thinking and strive for continuations not departures. I believe innovative art is freedom from tradition, but is good art only when it is based upon and founded in tradition.

When asked what inspired a particular work, I rarely have a definitive answer. Everyone and everything that touches my life inspires me and eventually affects my art. If I remain alert and sensitive to my personal preferences and goals, as well as the characteristics of my chosen medium, ideas usually come faster than I seek them.

Lazy Daisy, 2011, 35 x 22.

Tree of Life, 2011, 22.5 x 22.5.

Abide,
2011,
24 x 36.

Lisa Ellis

Fairfax, Virginia

www.ellisquilts.com

Artist's Statement

My work is spiritual. It is an act of worship that comes from my soul. Whether it's a piece of imagery that will have a clear biblical message or a piece that conveys a more subtle theme of God's grace and life's beauty and humor, my work is always inspired by my appreciation of our great and holy God.

I am drawn to the medium of fabric because of its tactile nature. It connects us to the past of grandmothers and mothers keeping us warm at night. The variety of colors, textures, and patterns in fabric provides the ultimate palette on which to create a piece of art — and as a mathematician, I am drawn to the calculations of the puzzle to make pieces fit within a geometric framework.

As my own designs emerged in the early days of my art quilting, I created a technique I call the "Lazy Landscape," which abstracts various backgrounds of sky, seasons, water, sunsets, forests, or meadows, providing a rich texture on which to place trees, flowers, or other representations of God's creations.

Through my art, I strive to make the world a better place. Whether making work for my place of worship, a hospital, a friend, or a traveling group exhibit, I always endeavor to communicate hope, grace, love, and peace.

San Diego,
2007,
18 x 36.

Glass Beach, 2009, 36 x 48.

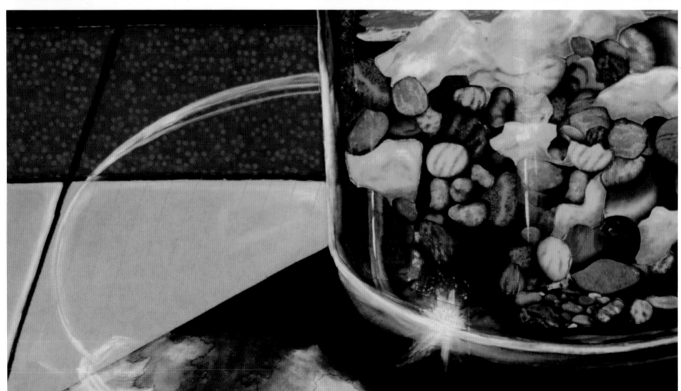

Desiree Habicht

Riverside, California

www.desireesdesigns.com

Tortured Soul, 2010, 36 x 48.

Artist's Statement

I began designing and painting over thirty years ago. I started my career in art as a watercolor artist and muralist and soon began to paint murals and faux finishes for interior designers. I soon found my niche as I helped designers transform ordinary rooms into fun, happy themed rooms. From pediatric offices to model homes, my distinct style and animated faces created a colorful, fun, and whimsical world. Many of my images are a blend of my fine art skills and my sense of fun and adventure.

I began my quilting career in 2001 after a family tragedy forced me to remain at home to care for my daughter. I have always tried to push myself to think and create outside of the box, so it was no surprise when I began designing and making art quilts. With my art background and my newfound love of fabric, I was excited about all the possibilities of creating a work of art with fabric.

I am passionate about my art and it shows in the things that I create. Art, in all forms, enables us to express ourselves; it gives us a voice and is very therapeutic. Many times my quilts tell a story; a personal story about an event in my life that other people can relate too. I love sharing my passion by teaching others the joy of creating art quilts, painting, and keeping a sketchbook journal.

The Journey, 2010, 41 x 54.

Gloria Hansen

East Windsor, New Jersey   **www.GloriaHansen.com**

Blushing Triangles 4, 2008, 40.5 x 41.5.

Creative Tip: *The biggest tip that I can share with other quilt makers is to be persistent in that which you want to accomplish. Be true to yourself and your vision. Ignore the naysayers. Everything worthwhile takes work and there will always be naysayers. Push on and be true to yourself and your vision.*

Artist's Statement

My passions include creating digital designs on my Macintosh computers (big time Mac junkie): quiltmaking and working with a variety of media such as pigment inks, paints, dyes, fabric, papers, and threads; and photography, using my cameras (Nikon girl) and printers (Epson junkie).

I did a lot of arts and crafts while growing up and in school studied graphic arts, photography, creative writing, and art. I am a computer nerd, specifically the Macintosh kind. In 1982, I took my first formal quilting class and I then went on to take every class on design and color that I could find.

I developed my unique techniques and learned how to paint, airbrush, and dye fabric. It didn't take long for me to start figuring out ways to use machines as design tools. I shoved fabric in various printers and copiers, and in the mid-1990s helped develop a recipe to make dye-based inkjet ink water resistant (that was before Bubble Jet Set).

Today my work combines everything I learned along my stitching journey. I continue to love photography and was an early advocate of digital photography. As a result, I have thousands of images from which to draw inspiration, if just for color usage ideas. I continue to design using software programs on my computer, I still continue to dye and paint fabric, and I often use acrylic fabric paint, color pencils, pastels, and other media directly on my prints to further enhance the color.

Nearly everything I make requires many attempts and persistence. My newer work combines geometric shapes with my love for photography. *It's Time* deals with my obsession with time — feeling like I never have enough, wondering if I'm wasting it, being amazed at how quickly it goes by, and saddened by what is now no more. It has a series of wavy lines over the design to reflect the ebb and flow of it passing.

The Journey is another piece that combines geometric shapes with photographic imagery. This one focuses on transitional places — tunnels, paths, doorways, trains, planes, and flying machines. Like *It's Time*, this work reflects time but in a transitional way: the going from one place to another. How a path may result in the same destination or a completely new one. How the unknown can be both frightening and hopeful.

It's Time,
2010,
57 x 47.

Refracted Lily,
2010,
27.5 x 20.

Squared Illusions 6, 2007, 34 x 44.

Painted Turtle, 2010, 15 x 14. Photography by Vickie and Paul Mathas.

Vickie Mathas

Mount Laurel, New Jersey   www.VickieMathas.com

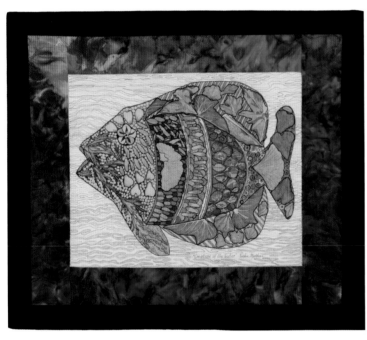

Gingko Fish, 2011, 22 x 19. Photography by Vickie and Paul Mathas.

Artist's Statement

I draw my inspiration from my surroundings. I try to capture the textures, colors, and lines hidden in nature's palette and beyond. Created images are the result of a rendering of natural and man-made materials. They evolve through a creative process that drives my energy to express my vision called "Totem Images." These are the objects and symbols I use to provide a more intimate awareness of our environment through my art.

Art quilts have become the medium of my artistic expression. Inspiration can come from anywhere in my environment. Once an idea has been formed, I then choose among an array of techniques and materials to complete each piece. The quilting process follows, as I select the fabrics and decide on the stitching that will best express the desired image, and then comes embellishment, which takes a variety of forms and methods. Finally, the piece is finished through binding, and a story is written about each piece, hand printed, signed, and sewn on the back. All of my work is then ready to hang.

I find inspiration from many venues, sometimes through photography, but often through observation and appreciation of the natural world. That is why many of my images are animals or botanicals. Others are a result of a challenge to create an image/ expression from an idea outside my practiced genre. Other artists can benefit from the understanding that the more techniques and media you explore, the larger your vocabulary becomes for expression. For me, it is the connection of line into texture. I have always had a strong sense of using line, no matter what technique or medium I have used.

To finish each of my art quilts, I reflect upon the image created by writing a short story about the piece and stitching it to the back. Writing this story also gives me a chance to think about the image and perhaps guide or inspire my next piece.

Reki Hands,
2010,
15 x 23.
Photography
by Vickie and
Paul Mathas.

Raven Wing Down, 2010, 14 x 16. *Photography by Vickie and Paul Mathas.*

My Creative Technique

One of the techniques that I use in the inspiration phase is called "flower pounding," where I choose flowers, grasses, weeds, and leaves from nature to create the shapes and composition for the resulting piece. I then draw on and around the image, adding my own patterns, colors, and designs. I use ink, paint, or colored pencil on the piece, which then is quilted and embellished. An example of this flower-pounding technique is found in my piece *Gingko Fish*. I started with a contour line drawing of a fish,

the cross cultural symbol of good luck, happiness, and abundance. I then looked for botanicals to complement the shape and texture of the fish. The gingko leaf was the perfect fit. The leaf itself is the symbol for longevity, hope, resilience, and peace. I also used morning glory leaves, dill, and other flower petals. I pounded these objects by placing them on prepared for dying fabric (pdf), taped down with masking tape, laid on a hard surface, and hammered with great force. The tape is then pulled off, leaving a botanical impression waiting for detailed painting.

Within Without, 2010, 23 x 30.

Cormorants Perch, 2010, 30 x 47.

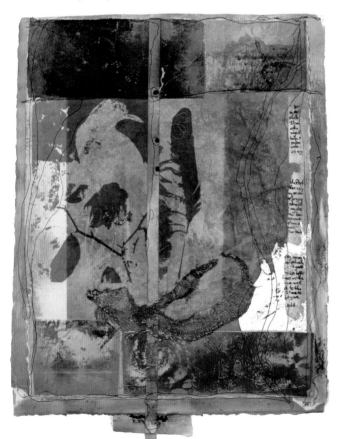

Whispers of the Positive, 2010, 16 x 23.

Wen Redmond

Rollinsford, New Hampshire   **www.wenredmond.weebly.com**

Artist's Statement

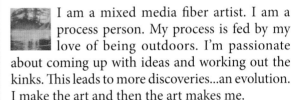

I am a mixed media fiber artist. I am a process person. My process is fed by my love of being outdoors. I'm passionate about coming up with ideas and working out the kinks. This leads to more discoveries...an evolution. I make the art and then the art makes me.

Part of that process is photography. My fascination with photography is finding expression by printing directly onto various substrates, creating stitched textural constructions. I call this work "Digital Fiber." I can see the most exquisite scenes or combinations of patterns and want to share that beauty. My art represents these moments, as they are what lie beneath. I bring them back to share, to remind, to remember. These moments become my source...my well. I hope to bring that energy into my art making, to communicate the positive.

Layers peeled back reveal the source, the inspiration, and my mad desire to capture thoughts, dreams, and the beauty of nature. Each work is individual and a communication between my inner imagination and later, the viewer.

Winter Tree, 2008, 26 x 21.

Holographic Fiber

My longtime fascination with photography is finding expression by printing directly onto various natural fibers. I have created an unusual photographic fiber art treatment. The work, when viewed, appears holographic or 3-D. To achieve this effect, I print my original digital images twice. I print on especially treated silk organza for the top image and mount the second image on polyester and rayon stabilizer backing. When mounted with fabric borders, the small space of the 3/4" stretcher bars allows the image to transform. Folks will walk by my work in an exhibit and often exclaim, "How did you do that!"

I use an Epson Stylus® Photo R2400, among other Epson printers. The UltraChrome™ inks are archival, water proof, and fade resistant for at least two hundred years. My pieces can include hand-dyed, painted, and surface design techniques, i.e. sun prints, stamps, photo silkscreen, and painted fabrics in the borders.

Waves,
2011,
48 x 18.
*Photography by
Atlanta Photography Center.*

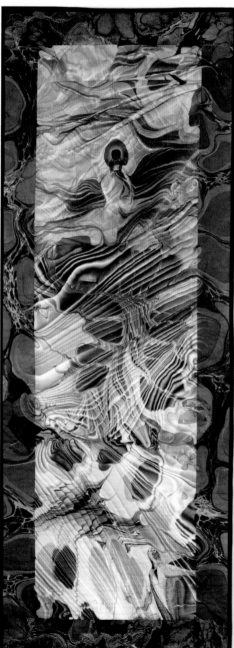

*Oil on Water,
2010,
20 x 50.
Photography by
Atlanta Photography Center.*

*Gulf Turbulence,
2010,
20 x 50.
Photography by
Atlanta Photography Center.*

Karen Reese Tunnell

Atlanta, Georgia

www.karentunnell.com

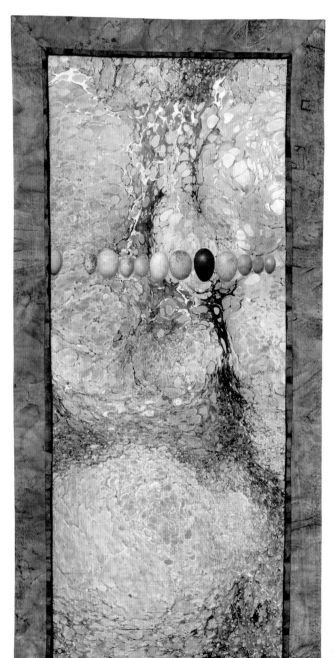

Artist's Statement

For more than forty years, I have been designing and fabricating art quilts and wall hangings. During that time I have taught textile art classes at a variety of schools, art centers, and museums. I attended art school, but learned traditional quilting in the mountains of North Carolina.

My recent work has focused on hydro-printing (marbling) and coloring my own fabric. Some is appliquéd and quilted while some becomes the background for hand-drawn images that are framed to display.

In April 2010, as I completed a series of hydro-prints on fabric, the *Deepwater Horizon* oil rig exploded in the Gulf of Mexico. Surrounded by news of the disaster I realized that my prints bore an eerie resemblance to oil floating on water. The traditional marbling technique, called Spanish Wave, creates the illusion of a wavy, three-dimensional surface on the flat fabric. In response to the spill, I began to draw plants and wildlife of the Gulf onto the printed fabric with colored pencil, pens, and oil sticks. There are fourteen pieces in the series. All of them express my fears about the safety of our fragile ecosystems and my hope for a quick and dramatic improvement in safeguards against future disasters.

Eggs,
2011,
20 x 50.
Photography by
Atlanta Photography Center.

Tsunami, 2011, 24 x 26. *Photography by Ian Betts.*

Meghan Welch

Fairfax, Virginia

meghanjwelch@yahoo.com

Spring Showers, 2010, 24 x 18. *Photography by Ian Betts.*

Artist's Statement

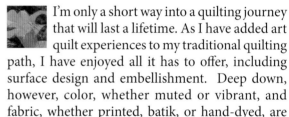 I'm only a short way into a quilting journey that will last a lifetime. As I have added art quilt experiences to my traditional quilting path, I have enjoyed all it has to offer, including surface design and embellishment. Deep down, however, color, whether muted or vibrant, and fabric, whether printed, batik, or hand-dyed, are my first loves.

My traditional quilting background often triggers thoughts of blocks and grids and I feel compelled to show only clean edges and perfect seams. Discovering a technique that distances me from such preconceived notions has been an important part of my art quilt experimentation. I have found that when I divorce myself from those notions and focus on the core aspects of color and fabric my art quilts flow more smoothly from concept to end result.

I am currently accomplishing this by cutting fabric into thin strips or small shapes and then layering them based on their color and value to create specific shapes or patterns. This helps me to think outside of the grid or block and focus on the overall design and effect. Some of my recent pieces feature this technique exclusively while in others it has helped create a focal point. I am savoring this point in my journey and look forward to discovering new design and construction techniques that work for me in the future.

Place in the World, 2009, 10 x 13. Photography by Ian Betts.

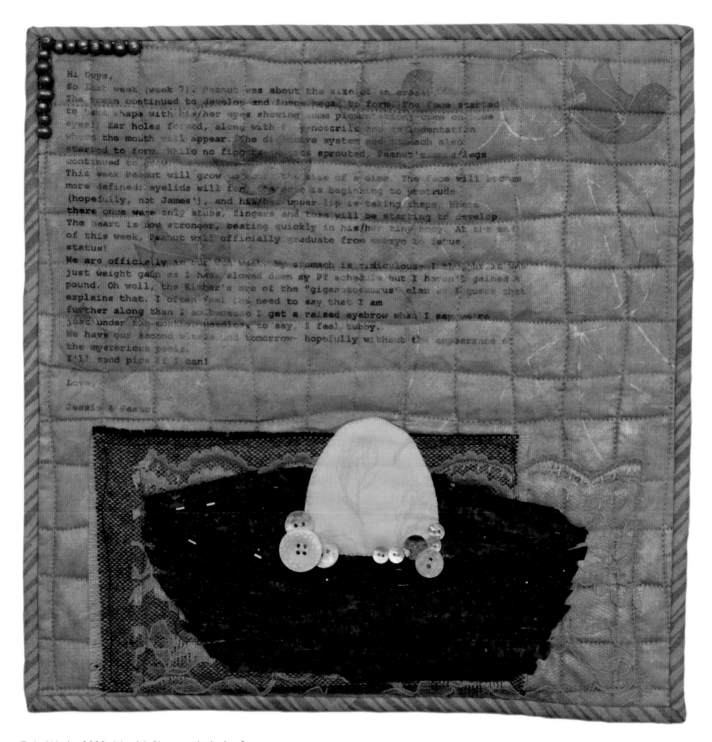

Eight Weeks, 2009, 14 x 14. *Photography by Ian Betts.*

Fusing Layers of Fabric

My fusing technique allowed me to create the illusion of expansion and depth gently swirling around a core center without complicated piecing and pattern drafting. I was able to use the hues and patterns of the commercial cottons fabrics to create a subtle effect where individual designs did not distract but added to the whole. I created *Place in the World* by layering 1/4" pieces of fabric with fusible on the back on top of fusible Timtex™. Using fusible on both the fabric and the foundation ensures that most of the fabric will be fused, even if fabric is layered on top of other pieces.

The most important design consideration is to identify early how the pieces will overlap so you can layer them accordingly. In this piece, I had to work from the outside to the inside to achieve a feeling of expansion. Working from the inside out (which I did first) created a whirlpool, or sinking, feeling since the angled exposed fabric edges were on the inside of the arcs.

Fireworks Flowers Ninepatch,
2010,
35 x 36.

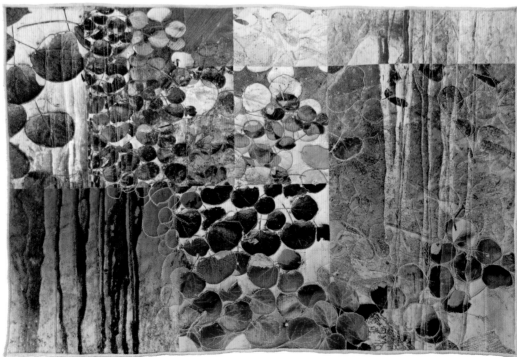

Autumnal Equinox #3:
Before the Frost,
2010,
22 x 33.

Charlotte Ziebarth

Boulder, Colorado

www.charlotteziebarth.com

Aspen Reflections Watercolor, 2009, 48 x 39.

Artist's Statement

The inspiration for most of my work comes from the forms, colors, and patterns of the natural environment. To explore the mysteries, the nuances, the magic, and the intricate patterns found even in everyday environments is my goal. I am constantly looking for the evocative photograph, whether sitting with my laptop or out walking, hiking, and traveling. I seek strong images that will become the basis for my digital transformations.

My work starts with the image a photograph can capture at a single moment in time. Once I start altering and combining images, I aim to highlight abstract patterns unnoticed at the initial observation. I also work with the interplay of color. Color makes me salivate. My work is often an exploration of color itself and how colors speak to each other. The result is often a fantasy-like impression where reality takes on a sense of mystery, but also communicates the beauty of the object or experience.

Printing my digital paintings on cloth allows me to take advantage of the textures and light reflecting the variations of different kinds of fabrics. The traditions of the quilter's world (the repetition of the stitched line, the patterning of grids and block arrangements, and the resulting bas-relief effects of stitched, quilted cloth) allow me to tell a multi-layered story of my impressions of the real and imagined landscape.

I feel that the artistic possibilities of software "painting" combined with the ability to print those "paintings" on any kind of fabric give the contemporary quilt artist an entirely new set of tools that we are just beginning to explore.

Reflection Ripples, 2008, 49 x 43.

Five: 3-D Designs & Embellishments

Some of today's art quilters are shopping in non-traditional places. We are browsing the hardware section, visiting thrift shops, harvesting plants from our gardens, raiding the button jar, and finding that perfect "thing" in the antique shop. The possibilities that arise when we move beyond the flat surface is amazing. Some artists have chosen to display their work away from the wall and allow the audience to see their quilt from all angles. Others have found unique ways to incorporate unusual items onto the surface of their quilts. The sparkle of beads and the excitement of embellishments makes my heart sing!

This small quilt was created in 2010 for the Alliance for American Quilts auction. It features a vintage block, creative quilting and lots of antique buttons. I love the tactile waterfall of the buttons as they cascade across the face of this piece.

Sharfall,
2010,
12 x 12,
Mary Kerr.

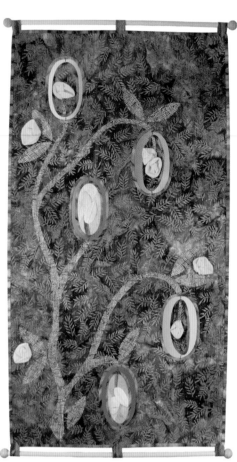

My Design Process

Perhaps the most difficult part of making a kinetic quilt is choosing the items for the mini-quilts that show a "happening" or event. Both sides need to "play together," but still provide enough difference to be interesting. Designing them is almost like playing 3-D games.

I make the bindings of the cut-outs on the bias. They're a single binding, cut about 1-1/4" wide and I have found that if I can use a fabric where the print or color of the fabric goes right to the finished edge of the selvage, then I don't need to turn the end piece under at the join and the binding looks much smoother. That creative "tip" would work for any miniature quilt.

Evening Primrose-Opening Night (front and back), 2006, 25 x 46.

Linda Cooper

Burke, Virginia　　　**www.LindaCooperQuilts.com**

Artist's Statement

Among the quilts I create, I like my kinetic quilts best. They're called kinetic because they use kinetic energy — a breeze, a touch, a vibration — to rotate certain free-hanging blocks within the structure of the overall quilt. The quilts can be viewed from the front or back; the rotating blocks create variety since each block is designed to work equally well with the front or the back as it rotates freely within its cutout space.

As with many creative leaps, the rotating block idea was the result of a simple experience from my life. My father was a fisherman and often requested fishing-lure swivels for presents when I was young. I was fascinated by them and always wanted to find a way to use them in a quilt to add a mobile effect. The quilt needs to be rigid to keep its form and support the rotating blocks. Timtex and Peltex® interfacings are excellent products that work well in kinetic quilts.

To further personalize my quilts, I like to include fabric that I have hand-painted. Sometimes I use sunprints that I have created using Setacolor and sometimes I play with the ombre effect you can get by moving from one value of a color to another value of the same hue or by moving from one color to a completely different color. I think ombres are undervalued in the art and quilting worlds and I enjoy using them whenever I can.

When Fish Party
(front and back),
2010,
22 x 23.

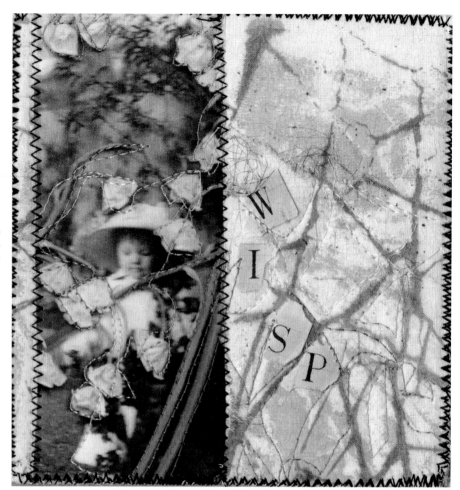

A Wisp of a Girl,
2010,
5 x 5.

Maddie's Dream,
2010,
25 x 20.5.

Lisa Corson

Bristol, Connecticut

www.homespunheritage.com

Artist's Statement

My art quilts combine many aspects of art, craft, history, and storytelling. I experiment by putting photographs onto fabric and combining them with other textures, patterns, and materials. For years, I have been collecting vintage photographs of families, children, and scenes of daily life. Each photograph contains a story of a life waiting to be told and I can't seem to pass up the opportunity to take home all these orphans. It seemed only natural that the physical warmth of a quilt should be combined with the emotional warmth of a story or personal history.

My fiber art cards and small art quilts meld together vintage photographs, handmade and commercial fabrics, poems, diary entries, love letters, and other artifacts of a life, such as buttons, keys, old tickets, maps, and other keepsakes. From these pieces, I spin a short vignette about the people in the photographs in the hope that the viewer's imagination will take it from there.

Up until recently, I worked in a very small studio space in which I created a nest of sorts of all of the tiny items I used to create my art quilts. Over the winter, I moved into a new, large art studio, and I have been growing and changing as an artist ever since. My work has become larger in size, and the new space has allowed me to really begin to explore and exploit new materials and techniques. Most recently, I have been exploring putting my traditional fine art training in disciplines such as drawing, painting, and print-making to use in my art quilts.

However, the collector in me persists — only now I am collecting a different kind of orphaned or abandoned item. I can frequently be seen looking at the ground when I walk, filling my pockets with shiny and rusty bits. These miscellaneous items are used to make impressions, imprints, or transfer color and texture onto fabric to be used in my art quilts, thereby preserving them and their history.

Portrait of Aldea, 2010, 5 x 5.

115

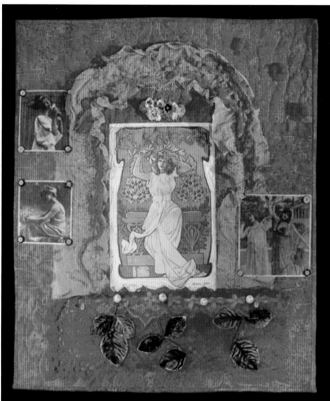

Audubon Swans,
2011,
18 x 18.
*Photography by
Miriam Rosenthal,
ThirdEyePhotography.*

Lady in Red,
2009,
18 x 18.
*Photography by
Miriam Rosenthal,
ThirdEyePhotography.*

Joan of Arc,
2011,
18 x 18.
*Photography by
Miriam Rosenthal,
ThirdEyePhotography.*

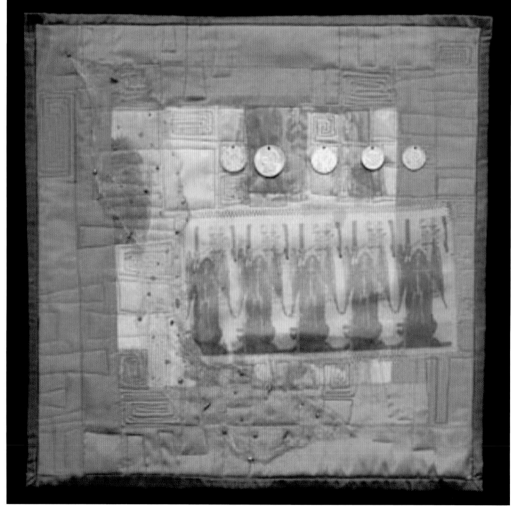

Judy Gula

Alexandria, Virginia

www.ArtisticArtifacts.com

Artist's Statement

I believe that to make art you must live art. Every day, I am surrounded by the things that inspire me, both at home and in my shop. I find inspiration in materials, my interactions with other artists, and in surprising and unexpected experiences.

My art comes from my experiences and from my circle of friends. I often work with vintage materials and they fill me with visions and ideas. The materials speak to me and I provide their voice.

There is no plan directing the creation of a quilt, only the materials. My quilts are assemblages of fiber, found objects, and treasured artifacts. I love to play with hand-dyed vintage trims, silk, and lace. Old pins, vintage photos, a fragment of an antique suitcase, a crumpled postcard, and buttons are all fair game when I start to create.

My goal is to share my love of art with as many people as possible. In empowering them to create their own artwork, I find my bliss.

On the Boardwalk, 2010, 18 x 18.
Photography by Miriam Rosenthal, ThirdEyePhotography.

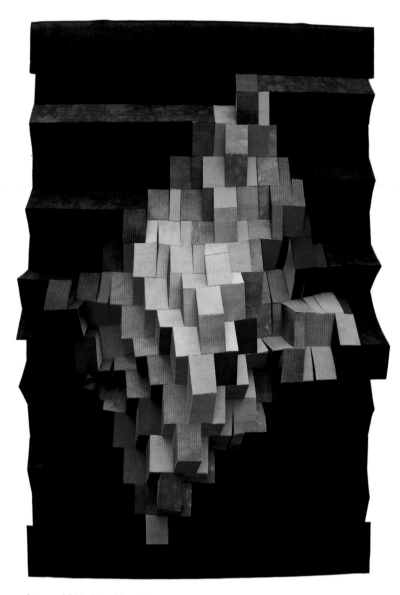

Vertigo, 2007, 27.5 x 27.5 x 3.

Spaces, 2010, 51 x 33 x 10.

Two by Two, 2009, 12 x 12 x 2.

Diane Nunez

Southfield, Michigan

www.dianenunez.com

Hanging my art quilts

Some of my work cannot be entered into "quilt" shows that require a standard 4" sleeve for the back. I do not think all of my work lends itself to that and find it very limiting nor does it give me a "creative opportunity." Some of the grid structures I have created are interesting by using one or two nails on the wall to hang them from. The drape created by this is interesting and if hung away from the wall creates more shadows. It is fun to send the work to a show and see how it will be hung.

Artist's Statement

 My chosen profession of Landscape Architecture involves elements of design similar to quilting, using the combination of color, line, pattern, rhythm, and texture. It also requires designing two-dimensionally on paper while envisioning its completed three-dimensional form. These same design components play a large role in my fabric constructions.

I find the tactile nature of fabric, thread, and embellishments intriguing. My work leans towards geometric designs, with a prominent repetitive grid structure theme. The open spaces in the majority of my work allow for the use of shadows for further enhancement. Color, texture, and the projection of the form in its surrounding environment invite the viewer in.

Traditional and innovative techniques appear in the work; the methodology of construction techniques is simple: If I can sew it together with a sewing machine, life is good and I am very happy. I like to experiment, whether it is with non-traditional fiber, hand-dyeing my own fabric, or adding unusual embellishments. The work is very labor intensive, requiring much mathematical accuracy. I have found that the medium of quilting has allowed me to experience unexpected and exciting opportunities creating three-dimensional fabric constructions.

*Abundance
Within,
2010,
64 x 66.*

Marlene Ferrell Parillo

Lincolndale, New York **www.marleneferrellparillo.com**

Artist's Statement

 We are each a product of our experiences and the choices we make in life are an ultimate reflection of who we are.

Some things, however, are not choices. I believe that the older a person becomes, the more likely it is that they have had to weather crisis situations and learn the art of surrender. Those times and how we process their lessons shape who we become in life. It is my intention to explore this link in the narrative of my artwork.

My ceramic sculptures and mixed media tapestries are visual storytellers of lessons learned and the realization that many of our lessons are common to others. I am continually surprised at how my particular experience, when represented visually, resonates with so many others. It is a reminder that we are all connected and how frequently we may be unaware of this fact.

I explore the common, the obvious, even the sentimental with a strong sense of reflection, hope, and humor. I use obvious symbols and work in a manner that is reminiscent of folk art. I am fascinated by the fine boundary between two-dimensional and three-dimensional space and I am continually exploring that difference while telling my stories.

Faces, 2008, 24 x 36.

Dream City,
2009,
60 x 65.

My Design Process

I have been plagued with sleep impairments my entire life. Because my artwork is about storytelling, this theme has come up repeatedly in my work. *DreamCity* was an epic undertaking detailing the anxious energy that surrounds me at night when I want to be sleeping.

I started with a rough sketch of the idea. Small sleep-related vignettes were drawn on cloth and embroidered. Some of the details were sculpted in clay and attached to the cloth with refractory wire that was fired into the clay. Beadwork was used to adorn some of the scenes and add texture. The piece was then sewn together like a patchwork quilt. The surface had to be sewn onto a large canvas to give it the stability it needed to support the weight of the ceramic pieces. Once attached, all of the separate patches were further embroidered to weave them visually to the surrounding pieces. Like dreams themselves, all of the scenes flow into other scenes.

Included in the imagery are common archetypical dreams — the flight dream, the death dream, the anxiety dream, dreams of home, and grief dreams. Some symbols were used as imagery as well. Lizards, for example, are symbols of dreams in Native American theology. I sculpted lizards crawling across the surface of the quilt. The frogs I have used as a symbol of my home and, of course, I had to include the dancing toilets that interrupt a good night's sleep at all the wrong times.

Stages of Grief, 2008, 50 x 40.

Cook is a Four Letter Word,
2002,
67.5 x 66.

Teddy Pruett

Lake City, Florida

www.teddypruett.com

Church Ladies, 2008, 64 x 61.

Artist's Statement

By third grade I knew I wanted to be a writer. I wanted to tell stories. I managed to write a bit here and there across the years, but then my life was overtaken by quilting. Like many quilters, I took the traditional road, struggling to match points and work with grain lines.

I tried to make good quilts. I tried really, really hard, but my workmanship was lousy. Triangles would morph into unidentifiable shapes and the seams wandered off wherever they wished...with total disregard for my supervision.

I solved the problem by giving up. I gave up patterns, I gave up rules, I gave up trying to do matchy-matchy, but then.... I decided that if I had no standards then nothing I made could be substandard. I returned to doing what I do best — telling stories — but now I tell my stories in fabric.

My writer's brain loves text — any form, any place, any style. I began collecting fabrics with text more than twenty years ago, no matter the source. Curtains, clothing, yardage old and new, dish towels, aprons — it mattered not. If it had text or an identifiable object, I grabbed it.

A trip through a thrift shop is a wondrous thing! My friend says I shop at places she would only go into with gloves and tongs! I sort the fabrics into groups: critters, transportation, places, food, etc. Occasionally a theme suggests itself and I'm off and running. Rather, off and sewing. An adrenaline rush takes place and I can scarcely cut and sew fast enough. It is a joy to create using recycled items.

I am sure that judges cringe at my quilts, and that's okay. They are trained to reward perfection — and my quilts are far from perfect. My reward comes from the viewing public: I can see tears in people's eyes when studying a memorial quilt. I hear them laughing out loud at *Cook is a Four Letter Word* and see them examining *Fractured Wedding Ring* to see if their own memories are there. I make stories in fabric...and people read those stories. How cool is that?

Fractured Wedding Ring,
2005,
72 x 59.

The Betrayal,
2003,
27 × 38.5.

Creative Tip: Don't take it all too seriously; this is something you do for fun, love, relaxation, whatever. Go easy on yourself. If I had fretted over perfection, I would never have discovered what I was really meant to do with quilting.

Also, don't be afraid of "used" fabrics. They cost pennies and aren't too dear to cut into. When buying thrift shop clothing, look at the labels. A thin, worn label means the item has been worn heavily. We don't want sweat or body oils in our fabric — throw it back in the bin. If the label is still stiff and crunchy, the item is fresh from the store and ready to use.

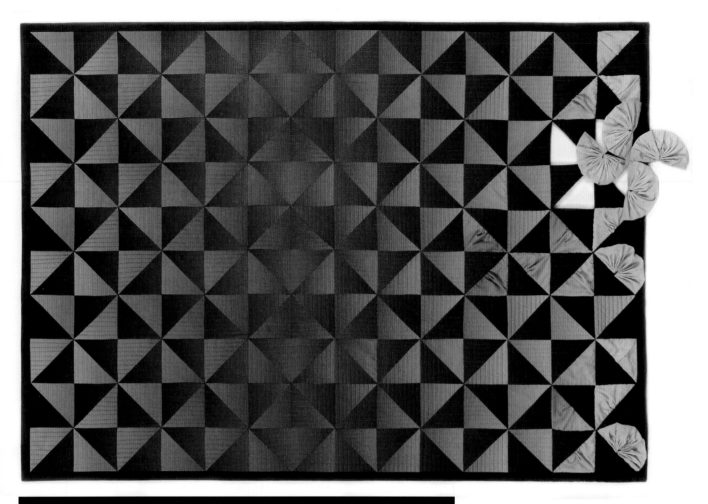

Pinwheel Evolution,
2010,
56 x 40.
*Photography by
Mark Frey.*

Trip Around the World,
2008,
36 x 36.
*Photography by
Mark Frey.*

Helen Remick

Seattle, Washington

www.helenremick.com

Artist's Statement

I have, at various times in my life, sewn, knitted, embroidered, needle-pointed, and crocheted. I love the feel of fiber in my hands. Quilting has been my focus since my retirement from the University of Washington at the end of 2005.

My mathematics background may have instructed my intrigue with geometrics. In my quilts, I prefer symmetry, mandalas, and spirals. Sometimes I begin my designs with a traditional pattern. Other times I may look to Islamic art forms. There is always some idea serving as an inspiration for design.

I work in overlapping series. Some series are by color while some are design elements — spirals appear frequently. My latest I call the "Prom Dress" series. I use fancy fabrics for the joy of working with them, yet do not have to worry about a date for the prom. What more could one ask?

I am currently obsessed with fabric yo-yos — I fuse fabrics in them, close them only part way, cut them in half, and make them in shapes other than circles — these are not ordinary yo-yos. Many are inspired by the names of Yoyo tricks, which on occasion are the same as the names of traditional quilt patterns (e.g., Trip Around the World and Pinwheel).

The change from more traditional construction to yo-yos has been wonderfully freeing. I have given myself permission to follow whatever fancy comes to mind. Most work out well, some do not. I learn something new either way.

Forward Pass, 2008, 50 x 44. Photography by Mark Frey.

Yo-yos

I took up yo-yos out of frustration. As ever fancier machine quilting became the focus of competitive quilting, I realized that I did not enjoy the process. Nor was I ready to buy expensive equipment that might or might not improve my machine quilting. Arthritis kept me from hand-quilting and was limiting my ability to do machine quilting whatever technique I used. I also found the process unpleasantly noisy; however, I would keep practicing in hopes that things would get better even though I knew they would not....

While I value keeping at problems, I also think it is important to know when to walk away. The description of quilts for the International Quilt Association shows requires that quilts be of three distinct layers and quilted with "three exceptions — Crazy quilts (which can be tied), Cathedral Windows-style quilts, and Yo-Yo quilts." Rather than persevering with machine quilting, I chose the "exception" of Yo-yos. It has been a wise choice for me.

Blooming Button Basket, 2010, 18 x 18.

Tulips from Two Lips,
2011,
18 x 18.

Didi Salvatierra

Abington, Maryland

www.DidiQuilts.com

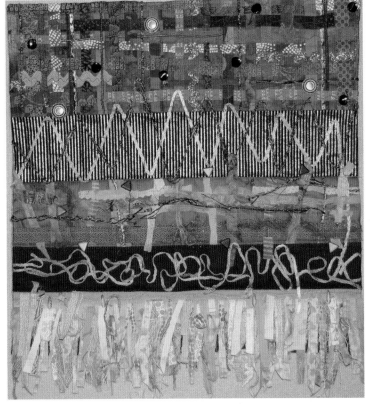

Salute Ami's Army, 2011, 16 x 16.

Artist's Statement

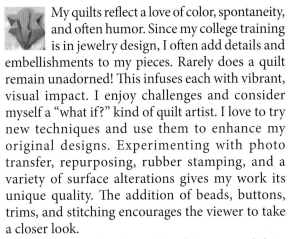

My quilts reflect a love of color, spontaneity, and often humor. Since my college training is in jewelry design, I often add details and embellishments to my pieces. Rarely does a quilt remain unadorned! This infuses each with vibrant, visual impact. I enjoy challenges and consider myself a "what if?" kind of quilt artist. I love to try new techniques and use them to enhance my original designs. Experimenting with photo transfer, repurposing, rubber stamping, and a variety of surface alterations gives my work its unique quality. The addition of beads, buttons, trims, and stitching encourages the viewer to take a closer look.

My appreciation for quilts of the past and their makers has inspired me as an artist. I admire the work of contemporary quilt makers and authors as well. In my own quilt art, I try to find the happy medium, combining some traditional elements with contemporary design, pattern, and color. The excitement of seeing a project completed never diminishes. I am fortunate to have found a creative medium that fuels my passion.

This woven border was just plain fun. I wove strips of batik over graduated solid color border segments. I couched white and black cording, added rick-rack over the satin stitched edge, and then carefully inked a small red convex sequin to resemble a ladybug.

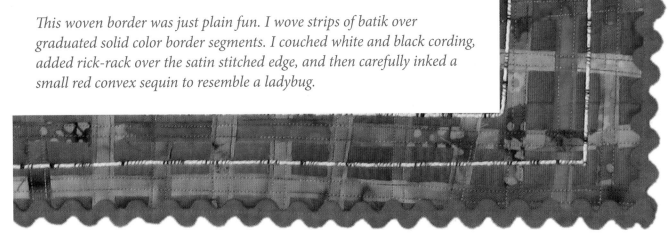

Goose Falls at Slack Tide, 2010, 30 x 42. Photography by Mike Travers.

Barbara Tinsman

Elkton, Maryland   **www.bitsandpiecesstudio.com**

Life Goes On, 2010, 41 x 34. *Photography by Mike Travers.*

Artist's Statement

The beauty, grandeur, and mysteries of the world around us are my inspiration regardless of the medium in which I am working. I am fascinated by the colors and the ever-changing light of the seasons, but those of us who live in urban areas may never experience the everyday wonders of our natural world. My work encourages viewers to enter the scene and think about the world portrayed and the role we play in it. What is the consequence of the action or event pictured? What will happen as a result of it? What would it be like if the event had not occurred or was substantially altered?

Fabric, threads, and yarns are my favorite creative media. They have been part of my life since I learned to sew in early childhood. With the exception of limited hand-dyes, my art quilts are constructed from commercially available fabric, yarn, and embellishments in multi-layer collage.

My Creative Process

To create my art quilts, I begin by transferring a full-size line drawing to petticoat netting with a permanent pen. The netting is pinned at the top to batting and backing. Each fabric in the collage is placed between the batting and netting and is outlined through the netting with chalk. Next the netting is turned back and the fabric is cut on the outline, allowing for overlap where needed. This process is repeated for each of the basic fabrics. Many layers of tulle and sheer fabric are layered on the basic fabrics until the desired effect is achieved. The whole quilt is covered with either black or gray tulle and each fabric is pinned or glued securely. Finally, the quilt is stabilized with clear thread and embellished with detailed thread painting using a Janome 6600 and Handiquilter 16. This method permits me to work quickly, freely make changes to the design as the quilt progresses, and to achieve a painterly quality.

I'll Have the Koi,
2010,
41 x 49.
*Photography by
Mike Travers.*

Flight,
2010,
42 x 24.
*Photography by
Mike Travers.*

Six:
Art Quilts from Photographs

Nowhere has the marriage of art and technology been more apparent that in the field of photography. The things artists are able to do with digital imagery and computer manipulation boggles the mind yet it is only the tip of the creative iceberg. Quilters have embraced these technological advances and created even more new and innovative techniques for us to try in our quilts. Can you just imagine what the future has in store....

In 2011, I was invited to participate in the "Power Suits" exhibit, curated by Cyndi Souder and Judy Gula. Each of us was given a packet of vintage suiting samples, buttons, and silk tie, and asked to interpret the theme of Power Suits. The result was an amazing exhibit of 105 small quilts that has traveled all over the United States and continues to excite audiences. My entry, called *The Power of a Dream*, features a photo of my father at his Doctoral graduation from Stanford University in 1967. He is pictured with his father who traveled from Kansas to help us celebrate the day. This was the first time I ever saw my grandfather wear a tie. Oh, the power of a dream.

The Power of a Dream,
2011,
18 x 18.
Mary Kerr.

Crimson's Last Stand, 2010, 16 x 24.

Flight, 2010, 42 x 24. Photography by Mike Travers.

Kathie Briggs

Charlevoix, Michigan

www.kathiebriggs.com

Artist's Statement

I find the inspiration for my art quilts in the flora and fauna of northern Michigan, where every season brings new wonders. We live on the shore of a woodland lake so I am lucky to be able to observe my subjects first-hand. I take a lot of photographs and while they are not art in themselves they do provide me with a reference for depicting my subjects.

I work with both my own hand-dyed fabrics and commercial cottons, mostly batiks. I begin, much like a painter, by creating a background. Occasionally a hand-dyed piece will provide the perfect background, but most of my backgrounds are pieced. My favorite piecing technique is to make 1/4" insertions into blocks, which I then combine to create a background that gives an impression of trees or grasses. Using my photographs as reference, I trace my drawings of birds and animals and then fuse the appliqué pieces on a sheet of parchment, which allows me to arrange them on the background. Generally, I free cut the trees, leaves, ferns, and other natural elements.

Heron on a Stump,
2010,
31 x 22.

Friday Night, Where's the Fish,
2010,
33 x 29.

Farmer Brown, 2010, 50 x 40.

Tanya Brown

Sunnyvale, California

www.tanyabrown.org

Artist's Statement

In early 2009, dissatisfied with the direction of my work, I began explorations that resulted in the fiber-based portrait series seen here. Although I had a background in graphic design and computer-based 3-D illustration, I never had a life-drawing class, and I had never been tutored in mixing colors. When I rendered people, the result was invariably grotesque, resembling radioactive elf/mutant hybrids rather than human beings. My goal was to tell short stories with my pictures, capturing the essence of a person's or creature's personality, and if I hoped to accomplish that I knew I had some work to do.

Happily, I've never been particularly intimidated by my own lack of knowledge. I decided that I would apply some elbow grease to the problem and learn to make a credible portrait. My first order of business was to experiment in black and white, using thread and smudged ink to emulate charcoal sketches. I then progressed to muted colors and finally to a bolder use of color and contrast coupled with dense, organic stitching.

During this two-year journey, I developed the process I use today, drank more coffee than I should have, and had quite a bit of fun. My designs are rendered in cloth, paint, and thread. They're illustrations in fiber, or stitched paintings, with visual texture and layers of meaning added in thread.

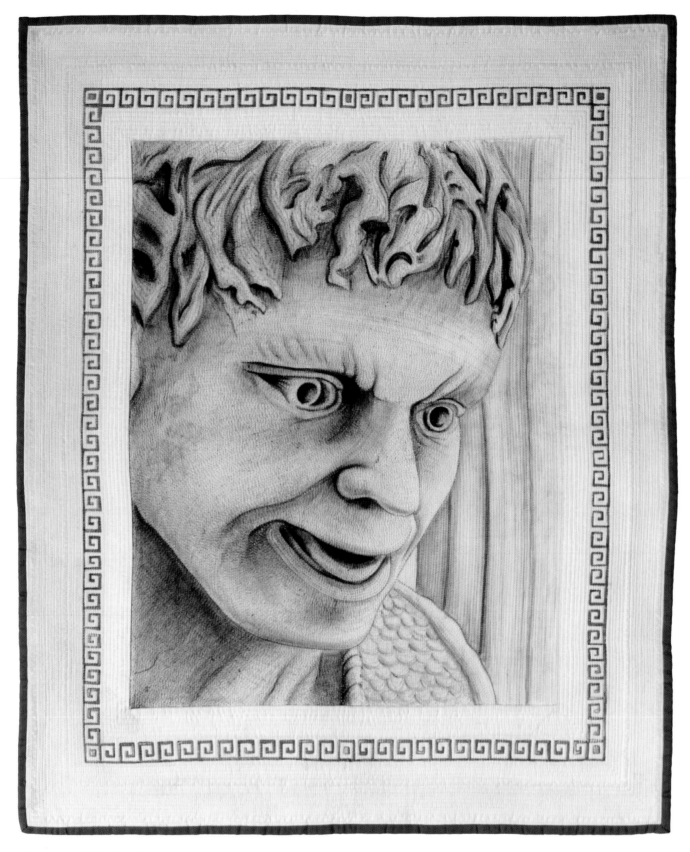

Creepy Boy, 2011, 24 x 29.

Creative Tip: The fretwork around the borders were created freehand with a sewing machine. This course of action is a swift path to madness and is not recommended to others. "Creepy Boy" taught me an important lesson: never stitch fretwork by eye. Life is short, too short for brain-numbing tasks that can be handled by a computer-controlled machine.

Siesta, 2010, 45 x 33.

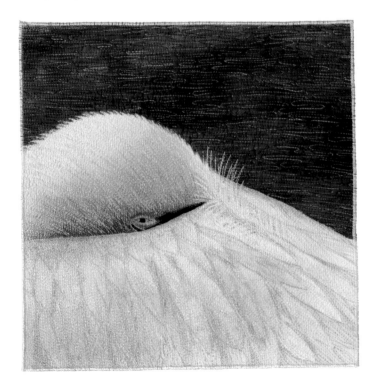

Suspicion, 2011, 11 x 11.

My Creative Process

Today my process begins with an idea or observation about a person or creature. I then make sketches of the desired scene and work out composition issues on paper. Often I'll go on a photo "safari" or stage a scene from which I'll take a variety of reference photos.

While consulting my layout sketches, I chop my reference photos to bits and create a photo composite in Adobe Photoshop®. The composite is then used to create a black-and-white "cartoon" in Adobe Illustrator®. After printing the finished cartoon, I trace it onto a length of soy-sized cotton and paint with ink or watercolor. (This is a technique popularized by John Marshall, who learned of it during his studies in Japan. The homemade soy milk not only acts as a sizing agent, but also bonds media, such as ink or watercolor, to the fabric.)

After sandwiching the resulting fabric painting with poly/wool batting, I quilt and then touch up the ink. My quilting style is naturalistic and very dense. The poly/wool batting provides the stability that is much needed with the varying densities and directions of stitching. An overlay of tracing paper lets me sketch and try out stitching ideas before making them permanent in cloth.

Pure Joy … Solitude, 2004, 30 x 37.5 (quilt and the original photo).

Wendy Butler Berns

Lake Mills, Wisconsin   **www.wendybutlerberns.com**

Artist's Statement

I love fabric. I love color. I love to stitch. Quilting is an art form that allows me to combine these passions. My quilts tell stories of people, places, and journeys that are important to me. The visions, feelings, and messages for these stories energetically dart about inside me.

Inspirations continually swim in my head. I use numerous techniques, but primarily I design and create my work using my "Picture Image Appliqué" process, which takes my visions from a photo or a line drawing through to the finished quilt. With my art quilts, I strive to create a special mood, as I work with my fabrics, dramatic value placement, captivating colors, and machine appliqué and machine quilting.

Photos of special places, beautiful garden images, and endearing family members and the stories behind them have been a source of inspiration for much of my work. I started working with my appliqué process in 2004 and since then have developed a large body of work by experimenting and exploring along the way. Most often, I am drawn to representational work, but have been stretching my design skills to work in more abstract ways as well.

By creating with fabric and thread, quilt making offers me the spontaneous freedom to express and direct this internal energy and vision into original, tangible, and textural images that I can share with others.

My Creative Process

For all of my Photo Album Quilts, I utilize my Picture Image Appliqué process. Since I have limited drawing skills, tracing simple lines from a photograph works well for me. Once my traced line drawing suits me, I enlarge the drawing to the size of the quilt and then the drawing is segmented out by my assigning pattern pieces and making tick marks. The enlarged line drawing pattern is traced to freezer paper; the freezer paper templates are ironed onto chosen fabrics. There is a glue basting assembly used and then finally the piece is machine appliquéd with a tiny zigzag stitch and monofilament thread, embellished, and machine quilted. It is a slick method that has allowed me to create picture quilts.

143

Pure Joy … Imagine That!, 2006, 51 x 51.

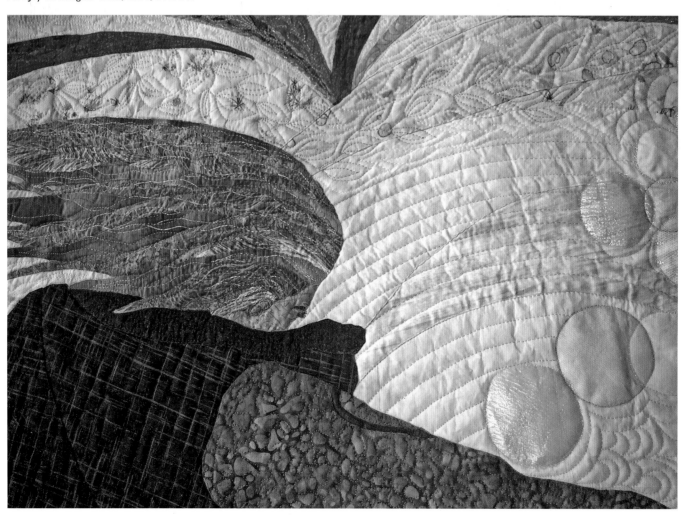

Tessellating Wings, 2010, 52.5 x 63.5.

American Gothic,
2010,
90 x 90.
Photography by
Howard Tu.

Hammer,
2008,
72 x 84.
Photography by
Howard Tu.

Luke Haynes

Seattle, Washington

www.LukeHaynes.com

2010, 2010, 86 x 86. *Photography by Howard Tu.*

Artist's Statement

My most recent works have been investigating nostalgia and function. I work with quilts because they embody these subconsciously while lending a unique materiality to the process and resultant product. I can work with disparate pieces of fabric and create a cohesive final product that is greater than the sum of its parts.

I am interested in taking a material with its own history and re-contextualizing it into something entirely new. This process of accumulation and layering offers a transformation of the traditional method of quilting, but also resonates with the ideas banding about in contemporary discourse on resources. The tag lines of "downcycling" and "upcycling" apply implicitly to this work, as clothes on their way to the landfill evolve into an environment, for people to reexamine the issues of comfort and waste, nostalgia and function, and art and craft.

I am interested in the choices we make to express ourselves to our world. The most apparent form of this is our clothes. We create an environment around ourselves to inform others how we desire to be perceived. By quilting with fabric and clothes I am initiating a dialogue between the immediate environments we create for ourselves and the environments we inhabit.

I often work with figural images. The human scale of quilts and fabric creates a dialogue with the viewer. I take these environments and create a larger space for people to exist within. As my work fills the walls, the quilts create a context for which people respond. The quilts then wrap the gallery and clothe the space rather than the individual clothing the self and entering the space.

Homesteaders,
2009,
72 x 54.
Photography by
Ken Sanville.

Wrapped in Tradition,
2010,
24 x 39.

The Mending,
2011,
20 x 30.
Photography by
Ken Sanville.

 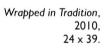

Lea McComas

Superior, Colorado

www.leamccomas.com

Bamboo, 2010, 34 x 47. Photography by Ken Sanville.

Artist's Statement

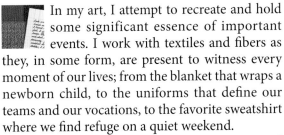

In my art, I attempt to recreate and hold some significant essence of important events. I work with textiles and fibers as they, in some form, are present to witness every moment of our lives; from the blanket that wraps a newborn child, to the uniforms that define our teams and our vocations, to the favorite sweatshirt where we find refuge on a quiet weekend.

Today, fiber art is exploding; there are a myriad of materials and techniques to be used. I find I'm easily overwhelmed by all the options, so my personal challenge has become: "What can I do with basic materials of fabric and thread? How far can I go with just these elements to create images that are compelling?" In striving for this, I find that my art is truly in my hands — it becomes about my skill, my creativity, my vision, and my ability to bring to life images that compel the viewer to stop and spend time with my art.

I find my inspiration from simple images of daily life. I love to be caught off-guard by the unexpected: the impish grin on a boy's face that leaves you wondering what he is thinking or the way shadow and light fall across a fresh bloom to further highlight its beauty. When an image startles me, I will create a composition using that image, which will, in turn, startle the viewer.

I know a piece is good when I see people walk up to view my work and it compels them to stop for a few moments, move in closer and perhaps hold up a hand or hold out a finger as if struggling with the urge to touch the piece, and then step back to view from a distance again with greater appreciation.

Anhinga,
2010,
42 x 27.5.

*Desert
Entertainer,*
2011,
39.5 x 30.5.

Barb McKie

Lyme, Connecticut

www.mckieart.com

Artist's Statement

Pelican Paphiopedilum, 2010, 28 x 30.

I started quilting before there were many books about the subject. I have never done a traditional quilt and instead invented my own way of doing my art quilts. I make pictorial art quilts based on my own photographs. I employ an unusual technique to print my images. It is the use of disperse or sublimation dyes to print to polyester fabric. It is a process I do myself that prints images to paper and then heat presses the image to polyester fabric. I chose this method because of the brightness of the colors and the resistance to UV light as compared with other methods of printing to fabric. Since the prints are limited to 16" x 20" because of my heat press, I usually fuse and machine appliqué overlapping prints to wool batting. I use trapunto to create dimension in the quilt by using several layers of wool batting in the raised areas and two layers of wool batting in the entire quilt.

I love to combine abstraction and reality in my work, and especially in my free-motion quilting that I do on my home machine and in abstracting backgrounds in Photoshop before printing. I also enjoy including humor when I can and a recent series includes combining orchids, which have much of the characteristics of faces, with animal eyes. I call them "Plantimals." In the last few years, I have been doing more animal art quilts and free-motion thread painting the animal's hair.

151

Starling of Botswana,
2009,
28 x 33.5.

Petunias on Parade,
2010,
47 x 26.5.

I travel a lot and take my camera with me everywhere I go, so many of my art quilts are based on my photographs of animals from around the world. However, they are also often from my own backyard as I study the squirrels, birds, and deer that frequent our property as well as the flowers I grow myself.

In the Glow,
2010,
20 x 16.

Early Birds,
2005,
49 x 38.

*Longhorn
Splashdown*,
2010,
47.5 x 33.5.

Ruth Powers

Carbondale, Kansas   **www.ruthpowersartquilts.com**

Artist's Statement

Much of my work is inspired by nature, as my daily walks fill my senses with color and design possibilities. My time in the studio results in pieces that hold those visions in fabric and thread.

I love working with commercially printed cottons, and the search for just the right material to portray a certain vision is part of the challenge, part of the fun! I am careful to use the best quality cotton fabrics and threads to ensure a long-lasting product.

For the most part, my work is pieced in the old-fashioned way, with no exposed edges. Seam lines often purposely do not meet, adding to the abstract realism of the piece. Most of the work is heavily machine quilted on my home sewing machine. Sometimes hand stitches and beading are added if the piece calls for it.

Colorado Kids,
2010,
37 x 44.

Foxglove Fairy,
2011,
41 x 42.

The Green Family,
2007,
24 x 18.

Original photo,
c. 1917.

Shannon Shirley

Woodbridge, Virginia   **www.onceinarabbitmoon.com**

Artist's Statement

Everywhere I go I see things that speak to my heart. They please me or make my mind wonder so photographing them is a way of recording possible ideas for future fiber art projects — the ideas are endless. The combination of colors, patterns, and textures intrigues me.

I love to choose the fabric, fibers, and techniques for my projects and let the quilts evolve as I work. Often the finished product is far different than the original idea. When I am creating, everything else just disappears...I get lost in the possibilities.

As with every other aspect of my life, my art is very eclectic. I am always open to learning new techniques and sharing the ones I know because creating and connecting with others are what bring me the greatest pleasures in life!

Garden Series #1, 2005, 20 x 24.

Garden Series #2, 2005, 20 x 24.

My Design Process

For the first quilt, I traced the basic shapes and some of the details onto the background fabric using a water soluble blue marker. Using Prang® crayons because they have more pigment in them, I colored the picture on the fabric. After the picture was complete, I had to wet it with water to rinse out the blue marker. When it was dry, I covered it with paper towels and ironed it with a hot dry iron to help set the crayons. The paper towels absorb some of the extra wax and pigment. I layered the fabric picture with Warm & White® batting and backing fabric and free motion quilted the flowers and the vase. The bead board was quilted with a walking foot and a narrow binding attached to finish it off.

Second in the series I used a fabric collage technique where the small pieces of fabric are dotted down with white glue and then covered with tulle to hold all the loose edges down before free motion quilting. Some of the shapes I cut free-hand and some I traced patterns for from the photograph. Actual floral prints were used for some of the flowers, but the majority are a variety of other prints to add interest. After covering it with tulle, I free motion quilted the flowers and vase using monofilament. The background detail was added with white on white quilting.

Garden Series #3, 2005, 20 x 24.

Garden Series #4, 2005, 20 x 24.

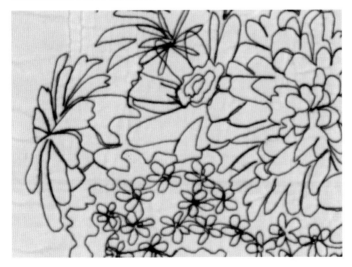

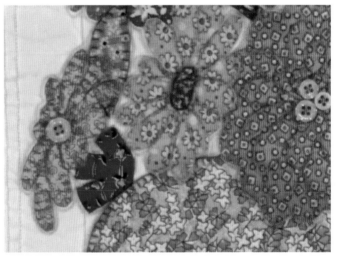

The third quilt was created by tracing the photograph onto water soluble stabilizer and then free motion sketching and quilting it at the same time using black cotton thread. Not all of the details were traced — some I just added as I stitched and looked at the photograph. After finishing the quilting, I had to wash away the stabilizer before the quilt could be finished.

I thought about making a quilt using the hand appliqué method, but my favorite method of appliqué is fusible, finished with hand embroidery. I also love 1930s reproduction fabrics, so the fourth quilt incorporates those techniques. When using fusible products for appliqué, I cut away the centers of the fusible so that the pieces remain soft and loose like traditional appliqué pieces. Blanket stitching the edges secures the pieces in place and adds texture and detail. I usually use two strands of embroidery floss and find I like the finished appearance. This quilt was finished with button embellishments and a narrow striped binding.

For a number of years the quilts were displayed together on a piece of leafy green batik background, but have now been separated into four individual quilts again.

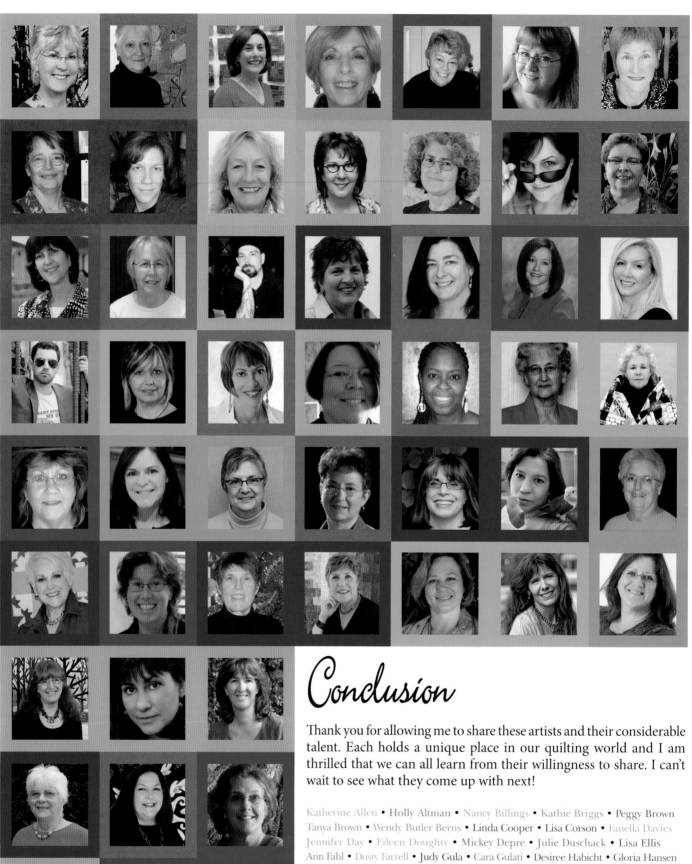

Conclusion

Thank you for allowing me to share these artists and their considerable talent. Each holds a unique place in our quilting world and I am thrilled that we can all learn from their willingness to share. I can't wait to see what they come up with next!

Katherine Allen • Holly Altman • Nancy Billings • Kathie Briggs • Peggy Brown
Tanya Brown • Wendy Butler Berns • Linda Cooper • Lisa Corson • Fanella Davies
Jennifer Day • Eileen Doughty • Mickey Depre • Julie Duschack • Lisa Ellis
Ann Fahl • Dusty Farrell • Judy Gula • Cara Gulati • Desiree Habicht • Gloria Hansen
Luke Haynes • Anna Hergert • Aryana Londir • Teri Lucas • Aisha Lumumba
Nita Markos • Marjorie Marovelli • Vickie Mathas • Lea McComas • Barb McKie
Diane Melms • Diane Nunez • Marlene Ferrell Parillo • Ruth Powers
Teddy Pruett • Wen Redmond • Helen Remick • Didi Salvatierra • Linda Schmidt
Maya Schonenberger • Shannon Shirley • Sarah Ann Smith • Cyndi Souder
Karin Täuber • Barbara Tinsman • BJ Titus • Karen Reese Tunnell • Mary Vaneecke
Meghan Welch • Charlotte Ziebarth